YOU'RE LEARNING
ALL THE TIME

You're Learning All the Time

Edited by
Pam Flynn
Chris Johnson
Sue Lieberman
Hilary Armstrong

SPOKESMAN
Nottingham: Atlantic Highlands

First published in 1986 by:
Spokesman
Bertrand Russell House
Gamble Street
Nottingham, England
Tel. 0602 708318

and 171 First Avenue, Atlantic Highlands,
New Jersey 07716, USA

Copyright © Spokesman 1986

This book is copyright under the Berne Convention. All rights are reserved. Apart from any fair dealing for the purpose of private study, research criticism or review, as permitted under the Copyright Act, 1956, no part of this publication, may be reproduced, stored in a retrieval system, or transmitted, in any form or by any means, electronic, electrical, chemical, mechanical, photocopying, recording or otherwise, without the prior permission of the copyright owner. Enquiries should be addressed to the publishers.

British Library Cataloguing in Publication Data
You're learning all the time: women, education and community work.
1. Adult education of women — Great Britain
I. Flynn, Pam
374'.941'.088042   LC1666.G7

Library of Congress Cataloging-in-Publication Data
You're learning all the time.
 Bibliography: p.
 1. Women in community organization--Great Britain.
2. Women--Education--Great Britain. 3. Community organization--Great Britain.   I. Flynn, Pam.
HV245.Y68   1986   361.8'088042   86-20199

ISBN 0-85124-438-6
ISBN 0-86124-448-3 Pbk

Typeset, printed and bound by the Russell Press Ltd,
Nottingham (Tel. 0602 784505)

Cover designed by Suzy Varty

CONTENTS

Foreword   9

PART I: Two Women
1. Connie   13
2. Mary   28

PART II: First Time Round
3. From Raising Awareness to Positive Action: 42
Opportunities for Intervention
Val Millman
4. Young Women and Work: Careers Officers'   62
Perspectives
Olivia Grant & Linda Moore
5. Why Work with Girls?   67
Judy Seymour

PART III: Fighting Back
6. Changed Lives: The Power of Community Work and   80
Second Chance Education
Barbara Hancock
7. Co-operative Learning with Women in Scotland   99
Alicia Bruce
8. Sweet Street Women's Courses: An Exercise In Positive   112
Discrimination
Deborah Trayhurn
9. Making the Rungs on the Ladder: Women and   127
Community Work Training
Hilary Armstrong

Afterword 137

Bibliography 143

Contributors 145

Acknowledgements

We wish to thank

ACW Trust
N.E. Co-op
Rothley Trust
Hadrian Trust
for assistance with funding this publication.

Thanks are also due to Marian Lockley and to Newcastle Council for Voluntary Service for typing and administrative assistance and, last but not least, to Chris Cherry, Lee Fairlee and Nicky Turnbull, who shared their thinking with us, as well as to all the unnamed women whose experiences have helped shape this book.

The Editors

Foreword

The idea for this book arose from the involvement two of us had in writing a chapter for another book on "Feminist Perspectives and Practice"[1]. In that chapter, we tried to make the link between feminist theory and community work practice as we saw it carried on around us. Amongst other things, we asked why certain areas of work of particular importance to *women* had been largely ignored by the mainstream of community workers to that date.

This book is the next stage forward from that chapter. We saw the need for a complete book, approached from a feminist perspective, on education and community work; one particular area which had received relatively little attention from community workers. We believe that *no* community work can or should be carried on without regard for the distinctive effects that a particular issue has on women, black people, people with disabilities and other groups whose disadvantage stems from the very structures of our society. This is, we believe, the first complete book to make the links between education and community work; we hope it won't be the last.

One of our principles in preparing the book was that it should reflect as much as possible ideas and practice flourishing outside London, for too much community work literature tends to ignore this and focuses very largely on what is going on in the capital. As we are a north-east of England based group, this principle has meant that much of what is included in the book has a strong north-east flavour. This has brought its own disadvantage: in particular the lack of any chapter written from black women's perspectives. We recognise that the book is, as a result, ethnocentrist; and we would not want any reader to assume that we are speaking for the experience of black women in Britain. We tried hard to find black women contributors, but the lack of much developed work with black people in the north-east at the time we embarked on this book, combined with our own lack of contacts with black women in other parts of the country, resulted in failure on this particular point. We much regret this, but we recognise that black groups may well have priorities other than that of contributing to a book of this nature. We hope that our omission will be rectified in the future.

What our contributors have set down is a spectrum of views and experiences of the way education impinges on their lives, and the lives of the women they work with. The chapters have been arranged in a certain sequence, in order to bring out their complementary and paradoxical content: "formal" education sandwiched between the informal learning experiences of community activists and the nonformal, deliberately consciousness-raising approach of adult educators; the strictures accepted by the Careers Service in terms of qualifying age for non-traditional training, set against the efforts of youthworkers and the Sweet Street workers to tackle precisely the limited expectations and lack of opportunities for young women. We intend the book to be read as moving through a number of stages. "What constitutes 'learning'?" is the question underlying the contributions by "Two Women"; followed by several analyses of what is wrong with current mainstream provision; and, finally, ending on a positive note — fighting back: a variety of ways in which women have sought alternative provision to enable other women to make up for their lost years. We, as editors, provide the Afterword, in which we try to bring all the strands together.

Almost three years from the time we began planning this book, the world has changed considerably. Women's Committees have sprouted up all over the country, and new forms of adult education have been given the seal of approval by the Department of Education and Science (DES), through its NIACE/REPLAN[2] Programme. Many community workers will be involved in these initiatives. But we need not to lose sight of what is happening to mainstream education, or to women's position in society in general. Education is a major determinant of lifelong opportunities, and its currently inherent sexism and racism, as well as the ways in which its resources are distributed and controlled, must be challenged at every level. We hope that this book gives some signposts.

Pam Flynn
Chris Johnson
Sue Lieberman
Hilary Armstrong
June 1986

1. Craig et al *Community Work and the State*, RKP 1982
2. National Institute for Adult and Continuing Education

PART I

Two Women

Introductory

The chapters entitled *Connie* and *Mary* are highlights from extended interviews carried out by Pam Flynn in mid-1983. The interviews focused on each woman's entire educational history, from primary school onwards.

Inevitably, transcribed speech may read a little jerkily. The text you will read has been edited in conjunction with Mary and Connie and contains the material which they found most important in their own consideration of what education is, especially in adult life.

The two women's experiences form the faces of one coin: Connie is North Eastern born, with only limited experience of the formal education system. Mary is a settler from the South with several "professional" qualifications. The commonality in their experience is of being women activists around housing issues, whose experiences of non-formal adult education with a critical edge to it has informed their action and their philosophy.

For the wider considerations of the book as a whole, housing is just one example of the many community work issues — transport, childcare, health, safe streets, educational opportunities, anti-racism — which abutt directly onto women's lives. This book is about thousands of Marys and Connies, and is for all of them.

CHAPTER ONE

Connie

I didn't mind school. I never ever minded school. Elswick Road was sort of a doddle because you went into prefabs for things like cookery and the likes which I enjoyed anyway. Then you went up to the old Bentinck Road school to do sewing and art. Then you had to go to Forsyth Road for hockey and things like that. There was actually quite a lot of excursions attached to that school. I'm not saying that it might have been different if we'd been stuck in the school all the time. Thinking back on it we actually spent quite a lot of time in travelling around. You know you had to walk up Bentinck Road to the school, that was all time off your schooling. You had to go to Forsyth Road which meant buses. You had to go to Bond Street baths for to do baths, so it just seemed to be that we spent a lot of time out of the school.

It was an all girls school. I liked it to be quite honest because George's Road wasn't — that was a mixed school and they used to do stupid things like putting your hair in inkwells, messing about and that — you know that was the daft kind of things they used to do to you. I was glad to see the back of half of them. I quite liked it just going to all girls. There wasn't the harassment except they did other stupid things, like as soon as you started to develop a bust, they automatically stripped you to see that you weren't stuffing your bra. That got right up my nose that part. We used to have baths as well. Because if you said with my mam working and the fire wasn't on through the day, you could have a bath in school. Of course you went in with your friend. You could have a half hour bath session. You got out of a half hour lesson that way. You did try to dodge.

I left school at 15. I didn't mind because in them days you had a job to go to. I mean it was nothing like now. Because I mean you used to have to go to the unemployment place, the dole, and you used to go for your interviews and I already had a job to start which I was quite looking forward to at Newcastle Wool Company. It was the first job I went after and I got it. I knew I had the job about the

February to start when I left school. I had a week off and then started work. I would have quite happily left school on the Friday and went to work on the Monday.

It was a shop assistant but you used to make rugs. They used to send orders out and people used to write in for wool, cash on delivery. So you used to put them up and put them to one side to pack — the packer used to pack them and when that work was done, you used to serve in the shop, in between times, if anybody came in the shop. And then you used to sit and make rugs. I loved that. I did a circle, and once I did a cloud which was a half circle and three shades of blue and I did one for a child's nursery with a rabbit and a tortoise. It was yours, you got your canvas, the canvas was all printed like, you got your wools, picked the colours and you did it. Nobody else touched it. You had to bind it and everything yourself. Everything was done by you. I would love to do it now, but it is very expensive. I mean if anybody said they would like one done, I wouldn't hesitate. I'd say you buy the stuff and I'll do it. It's soothing. You can talk while you're doing it.

I stayed at Newcastle Wool Company until I had my baby. I had Eddie two days before my 17th birthday. I worked all the time because I could stay at the back sitting down. I would have stayed on probably until I was a fortnight before if I hadn't had an accident at home at 6 months.

Adult Education

I went for typing and shorthand up to Pendower, that school where I used to go. My friend was going from work and she asked me to go with her and I thought I would like to. So we both went, and then I stopped going because I was having Eddie.

There didn't seem any point because after you'd done a full day at work which was 9 till 5 and you're expecting; it was just too much. I was always sorry I didn't go back. I think I should have done because I was just getting into it you know. I thought my education was finished when I left school at 15 and for the short time I went up to the Adult Education Centre and had to pack that in. We could of stuck at it, we could have made a go at it.

Beginning Community Action

I first became involved in the tenants' movement 9 years ago, maybe a bit longer. It was to get Noble Street pulled down, to get out of Noble Street to be more accurate.

I came to live in Noble Street because my marriage had broken up. I let him have the flat and I went into Kenilworth Road tenemented building. It was alright, I quite enjoyed living there because we had one of the better tenemented buildings. We all took turns in doing the stairs, the stairs and the marble were always nice and clean. I mean when we went there it was in a right scruff state but we got the bathroom and all that cleaned and got the other tenants, because some other women had come in, and we did a rota that we did the stairs. There was a good co-operative spirit there — we all liked it but what happened was — we used to pay our electric in meters and the landlord used to empty it and then it got disconnected so we went to the electric company and said look here we are a tenemented building and we've paid for our electric. I mean he came and emptied it every week when he got the rent and they said they can't help that. So we went down to the Civic Centre and Noble Street was all we got offered. They gave us the keys for there. We were paying £6 for 2 attic rooms and Noble Street for 3 bedrooms, separate bathroom and toilet, sitting room and kitchenette was only £2. 17s. 6d., which was half of what I was paying.

So I went in there and it was quite alright. This was May 1967. I was on one of the smallest blocks and I'd lived there before. My mother had lived in Sanderson Street so I knew everybody so I was back to where I was.

Noble Street was not as bad then. It deteriorated. I was in there for nearly 8 years. They started to give them to anyone, you could get off the train from Timbucktoo, say you were prepared to take Noble Street and they just gave them out and they had a floating population which was people coming in, getting the key, never doing anything with the flats, getting catalogues and hire purchase and taking a shoot so that we couldn't get hire purchase or anything. It got to the stage at the latter end where they wouldn't even put a rental TV in because the movement population were the ones that were taking the shoot with the televisions as well. It was them that really ruined it. It wasn't the hard core Noble Street tenants, the ones who had been in from the beginning, the ones who actually used it as their place to live. They weren't the ones who got it blacklisted as far as TV and hire purchase firms were concerned. The people who were left there were the ones to suffer because you couldn't get anything. It didn't matter how good a payer you were in full employment, and it got to the stage that you couldn't even get a job when you said you came from Noble Street. Because the building had a slump on and I tried to get a job to try and help Paul. Couldn't get one anyway and the Savoy was starting staff and I put my mother's address down and I got a start straightaway. A friend of mine who lived in Noble Street tried umpteen times to get jobs and was always refused and he did exactly the same thing as me. He went to Vickers and put down his mother's address at Walker and he got a start and he argues the same, he tried for 4 different jobs and yet as soon as he changed his address he was employed.

* * *

The Community Development Project which is now the West End Resource Centre had set up on Adelaide Terrace. They came down and asked the tenants if they wanted to get involved in getting out. At first I wavered, I thought it's not me, but then different associations had started, they had had the block by block representation and they got houses. It was then I realised that Eddie was going to go to Slatyford School and he was assumed to be this big hard kid, when in fact he's as soft as clarts and still is to this day. He wouldn't have coped with Slatyford coming from Noble Street so I thought oh well I'll give it a shot and I went to the meeting. After a while I got the Chairperson's job. Nobody else would take the job. By then the first big public meeting which was on the 14th January was coming off. We had all them Housing Department people coming. They said they would do what they could and we had to set up a special group and they also set up a project office to deal with just Noble Street and they promised they would get us out. They said it would take 5 years. Of course it didn't. Once it got started, the main people were out — the main bulk of people were out within 18 months.

There were some Polytechnic students doing a report and the papers took little bits of it and put it together. It came across in the *Evening Chronicle* as though the children were faceless and depraved, and played tiggy with hatchets, so we got a mini-bus down and picketed outside the *Evening Chronicle* and people came from McCutcheons Court because they were going through exactly the same. Slanderous accusations in the paper, really bad publicity and we said to the fellow that had done it 'have you ever been in Noble Street?' and we were amazed to find that he hadn't, he didn't even know where Noble Street was. All these reports were coming under his name and he didn't even know where the place was. So Kestrel had started — that was a children's project. I was also chairperson of that and the students had come to ask us if they could work with Kestrel and we said well could we have a look at their report which was on housing conditions in the area. In it they had on tape councillors saying if that councillor had their way, because they wouldn't say if it was a man or a woman, that they would build a 12 foot wall around Noble Street and go down once a week and throw bread at them. The students wouldn't identify the councillor so we didn't work with them.

We did things together in Noble Street, I mean we were all in the same boat, so if you had something to sell, if you'd managed to buy a 3-piece suite off someone else and you had something to sell it was all sold within Noble Street, or given away. If anybody had to go into hospital, it was nothing to take the pyjamas off your kids and lend them to somebody because they needed them. If somebody was confined to bed, in labour, because then you could have your children at home, it was nothing for you to lend your spare sheets because they were needed through the night, or your blankets. I mean there were two sorts of people in Noble Street. There was the people that lived there and would do anything for each other and there was what we classed as not worth a light, who were just using the place as a stop-gap. And then of course you had the element that didn't care anyway but most of those were people they had put in from institutions. You know this campaign was coming out to get people out of mental institutions and that because they shouldn't really be there. They were more backward than insane. We got quite a few of those. They weren't any bother but obviously because they had been in institutions that long they weren't as turned on to doing their windows and things like that and you used to have funny rows. Plus there was the element that you get in every estate, the thieves and that. But I mean I've got to admit I was there 8 years and I worked in the bingo every afternoon. My house could have been burgled anytime but I never got burgled. I never had one break-in. It happens all over. Take middle classes who own their own houses on very posh estates, you always get the odd house that is in disrepair because they won't look after it and untidy houses and dirty houses aren't just a problem of the working class.

The Community Development Project's Role

They weren't going to baby sit us. They told us, this is what we could do and it was up to us if we wanted to do it, but to do it we had to be there at the front. They could give us any background information. They could help us with our ideas. They would help us get them on paper. They would go through it with us but they weren't going to do it for us. They said that's it, you've got to go to the meetings. We used to go to these big meetings in the Civic Centre. So if we were there and we wanted to have our say we had to, there was nobody there to kick us and say 'come on, get a move on' or anything like that.

They made us very self-sufficient so that if we were caught on the hop by a report or by the housing, we didn't need them to hold our hand. We certainly needed them for the background information and for the moral support to keep on saying well you can do it, you know what you are talking about, you are living in it. Phoning the papers and things, they would sit in the same room but you would have to dial the number and you were the one that would have to say 'this is what's happening'. You know, 'we're having a meeting on the 16th in the Cushy Butterfield ... so and so's present'. But you had to do it. They'd always be there if you wanted to run things through but you had to be prepared to do it yourself.

How the Campaign Succeeded.

We never let the rest of the tenants down in Noble Street. There was a chance that the strong ones would get the houses first. So I said what we would do was that though we'd all fight individually to get out for our own families' sake, we would also fight for everybody out. If anybody got an offer they couldn't refuse because it was a nice house on a nice estate and that, then we would still stay together until everybody was out and we kept that promise. It was either the tenth or the eleventh one that I got but we had made the commitment that if the strong ones were rehoused, that we would serve out our term elected and then we would still stay on as the people to give the other people the information and the support. I mean I was sitting doing documentaries in my house in Wolsington Walk for Noble Street, eighteen month to two year after I was out because they thought I was the best person to do the speaking and I did that.

It's alright sticking up for tenants but you have to admit the bad as well as the good and it's just in most cases if you want to help the good, you have to help the bad as well because you can't say right 'we've got 75% good tenants on Noble Street. We'll fight for those 75% to get out and we'll leave the 25% thats not worth a light here.' We wouldn't have won. We had to take everybody along and just bite our tongue, you know.

Noble Street was really a perfect example of what tenants can do if they stick together and just argue on the truth, not fancify it or add to it or things like that. Just stick to the truth and stick together and using the media and getting people's support that you can do it. So it tends to be that groups and that have had the same kinds of problems that we had. Groups have started, people moved, getting out, then they tend to call on me because of my experiences in Noble Street to go and talk to the groups.

I went to the first lot of meetings travelling away for the first tenants' charter. But I had to stop going because I was expecting David and they advised me not to travel. So naturally I dropped out then and didn't bother going anymore to the Tenants Federation. Then, it's two year ago since the rents thing started. I got a letter from Loadman Street tenants asking us to come to an AGM, where they would be discussing the rent rises and I got back in from there. The trouble is when you're known and show your face. You're back in circulation again.

Activism and Women

The way I looked at it, it was alright for a man to say 'Oh well'. I mean he could go out to work in them days (because there were jobs in them days). Most men that were going out to work and that would come in, they would have their tea and that and they might watch the telly or they might go out for a pint. But a woman was stuck there all day and women in most North East houses are the ones that have to worry about laying the money out. Say you want a nice 3-piece suite and that and when you couldn't get hire purchase in Noble Street, then you had to put money away so that if you wanted to buy second hand or buy new, you would have to pay cash and it was because I wanted to be away from it. I mean I was one of the lucky ones, I had a good club man who I could get hire purchase and that from. I mean I had fitted carpets, I had new 3-piece suite, I had all my ceilings tiled but that was because Paul had a job. There was people who couldn't do that, people who didn't have jobs and were on supplementary benefit. But because I was there I was the one who thought I'm ashamed to tell anybody where I live. It doesn't bother fellows — their address. But if you're at the shops or sitting in the housy (Bingo) or somewhere like that and somebody says where do you live and you say 'Noble Street'. Oh that was it. You know they just automatically assumed that you were some flea-ridden, dirty object who never had a wash and didn't pay rent and whose kids went around playing tuggey — well they said tiggy, that's how illiterate the reporter was — tiggy with hatchets. It was stupid. There was no child on god's earth that was faceless and depraved. It didn't matter what slum they came out of.

I've been involved in some way for ten years but it doesn't seem that long when you reckon up. A lot of the women got involved anyway more than men because men are out at work all day and if you're going to the Civic Centre — they tend to be all day meetings and you can't hardly expect a man to stop off work to go and sit in the Civic Centre for a few hours. Half past two meetings for a woman who is going to collect her children from school is a bit ridiculous. Half past nine meetings are a bit ridiculous because by the time you get the kids to school at nine o'clock and run for a bus to get into the Civic Centre, they don't gear the times of the meetings really for proper involvement. You always seem to be making the push to arrange for to get the kids to be picked up, arrange for somebody to be there. Like Housing Management which can go on until four o'clock, after five sometimes. If you've got kids coming out of school from quarter past three, you've to work your life, organise your life around meetings. You know, when you clean up, when you've got to go to the shops. You shop days in advance. If you've nowt to do on a Monday, you do the shopping as far as you can so that you've got stuff in. I never used convenience foods until I got into the tenants' movement.

Community Action and Education

The first time we went out as a sort of educational thing was when the Sunderland Tenants' Federation was kicking off. They planned out for themselves like night time courses which were to last about ten or eleven weeks. They weren't education department courses and what they did there was that they went through everything. How you start a tenants' association, why you start, the posters and doing leaflets and all that kind of thing. At the end of it you actually had a playrole where somebody played a lady of ill repute on the estate and somebody else was a nattery old pensioner who was complaining and then you had the officers and the councillors and the chairperson of the group because they had this meeting for things and you worked it out. You had the plan of the estate and that and you knew where you lived on the estate and everything. We gave the Sunderland tenants our experience and of course we learned things that happened there.

Then after that, of course, it was doing the video. I was asked by some people down Walker to come and do a video, to talk about Noble Street on video. And that still gets shown now. It was only shown about a fortnight ago when we went to Walker Area Housing Management.

They were asking us questions on Noble Street and saying things like councillors are no different to you, just stand up and speak your mind. Don't let them put you down. You've got to go and talk to them kind of people when you feel strong; "you're rubbish and I'm better than you". It's no good going if you're not well because they just walk all over you. I think if you are a bit off colour you don't have the mental ability to stand there and battle which you can normally. Like when I once said 'Haway I'm just wasting my time here'. The Chairman looked at the Director and said "did you hear her!" They were flabbergasted but we weren't getting anywhere. That's the kind of thing that keeps you going. You think, classic, we'll put one over on you. You just have to watch for the next time it happens. I think you've got to laugh at a lot of it. I don't think if you haven't got any sense of humour, you could stick it because its alright riding high when your winning but there's more times you don't win. Their attitudes towards you — you've got to be a strong willed person to go back when you know for a fact that you're being patronised. That they are putting up with you to make the Labour Party look good.

You think all the time 'Do you think I'm daft?' Do you think I believe all the rubbish you're telling me?' You know you just have to come away and mentally talk to yourself because they would be quite happy to pull all the tenants in, cup of tea and a biscuit and isn't it nice and how's the family and little personalised phone calls — "Connie, I would like your idea on this". All the time they are just trying to get you away from the tenants. We stopped having a chairperson because if you get a chairperson that's sucked in, they can come and push their ideas on the rest of your committee. That annoys the Council because they say that sometimes they have to have a quick response. I say you don't have to have a response that quick. I can put the phone down and get people's opinions and we'll give you that but I'm not standing on my own. Like for the Tower Block meeting. They just wanted to meet with the Tenants Federation and not the rest of the Tower Blocks residents. We stuck out. I mean it was really getting them ratty. Why should the Fed meet them? There's not one person in the Fed lives in Tower Blocks.

Weekend Educationals

The trips we had to Leeds were very good because there was creche facilities, so the first two I went to I took the kids with me and they were well looked after. What it is, you go all over the country and you only ever get the chance to go in, go to the meetings, come out and set off home again. You never actually meet the people, you never get to see the houses, to talk to people about what the houses are like or what their councillors are like. Are they any better than the ones we've got? At the weekend school, people came from Glasgow, from Leeds, from Sheffield, you had time to do what you were there for. The first one was just to kick off why you got involved and everything. Then the second one, it went on to the unions and the Labour Party. The third one was what you expect to get out of it and what's your direction for tenants. So you do that through the day and you're still with the same people at the night time and you're not talking about the kids and that because obviously you're talking about what's been said, what your opinion is of how it's going. Then you get into the things that's happening on your estate and what's happening in their part of the country where they live. I think when we do things, when we go away to meetings and that, we should go earlier, even if it's just a couple of hours to have a look at the houses of the people that we are meeting. And all that comes out. I mean there was a lady from Scotland who actually brought it out and said 'I've been here since Friday. Its now Sunday and I'm going back to Scotland and I've never seen Leeds'. She was quite right. It's sharing experiences, finding what tenants have had the courage to go into court and if they've won and what would be the best way to handle things, like the national anti-dampness.

They are taking the council to court for section 99. They are taking out injunctions and when they got these little hitler officers coming and trying to talk the tenants out of taking the action, they then decided they would treat the cases like a divorce, "you don't talk to me, you talk to the solicitor", to get the little hitler officers off the tenants' back. Now you wouldn't know that if you weren't meeting the people from there and it's all sharing, it's all learning because then you can use that.

Like when we went to Glasgow as part of the anti-dampness group. They had a conference up there on housing. They've got Red Row multi-storeys — 30 storeys high with outside insulation. When we had this public meeting at Westgate Court, I said to the fellow from the Civic Centre on insulation "Have you ever thought about insulating from the outside?" "Oh" he says "we've only done it 7 storeys high in England. I've been to Germany mind they've got them 24 storeys there". I said 'Well you've never been to Glasgow, they've got them 30 storeys up there and different colours because its sort of a plastic'. I said 'Why haven't you gone there? You're disrupting all the tenants, they've got all this muck, they've got to get two weeks free rent for all the insulation and that going on'. They can't insulate every wall anyway. They're not going to pull the bath out and insulate the bathroom and that which means the cold air is going to get condensation on the internal walls and the same in the back kitchen. The walls are not going to insulate there. Yet they could get all over that if they decided to go and have a look at Glasgow or even to ask Glasgow how's it working. Yet the tenants know because the tenants have been.

Organising the Educationals

The first one where it was organisation — it was all work that we had done. The tenants from here and from Leeds and that had a meeting and they decided from that meeting what the weekend schools would be about. Then obviously there's a lot of things that we can't do because we're not trained to do it. Like getting the information, where to get it from, how to get reports and things, what kind of report is needed. The basic things are there and they can be used again. The same as on the day schools organising. All that stuff is there so if you have a group in another part of the city who wanted to do it, they could actually come and get that and change it to whatever suited them. But the basic format of how to run that day school is there. The same with the Tower Block day school. It's there forever because it's been written up. The same should happen with the weekend school. That will all be put together and it could be done again with different tenants. Because there was a mix of tenants like myself who were in on it and chairing the meetings, chairing the workshops, there were tenants who had been in it for a while and there was also new tenants. They found it fantastic because they were new tenants just getting there themselves, they had all these people they could sit and talk to.

There were people there from Newcastle, Sheffield and Scotland. Wigan, there were some from Wigan and from Laygate because they'd just got started there. We decided that we would have old and new so that there would be a mix. If you get a school with a lot of new people, then there's nothing to draw into the argument you know, or get people to talk about because they've never done nothing and they just sit looking at one another. We took a good part in that one but then the following one which was the councillors and trade unions, we took more of a part from sitting in the audience and asking questions but we monitored them. You were given tasks to do and so you got the people drawn together in the workshops because the workers didn't sit in the workshops. It was the tenants. The workers came around to see what was happening but they didn't actually sit in and run the workshops. And I missed the last one because I was ill but they reckon that was even better. I mean they said at the second one that that had made them think with the trade unions and the councils. You had this problem how would you tackle it by bringing in the unions and you had to work out your plan of action. The reports back from the last one had said they found that one even better. That was on the Government's policies and that. It was hard, it was hard on the mind but they'd actually enjoyed it.

Getting away from the house, you're not worrying about making the beds, having to run around doing the shopping, getting the house and everything done. You can concentrate on what you're there for, which is to talk and to share experiences and to gain knowledge. There wasn't the harassment of going back and forwards having the kids looked after. I mean even if you go away and you leave the kids at home you've still got the worry of what they're getting up to. Are they in and things like that? If you have them with you, you know where they are and at night times you've got them and you feel as if you can concentrate on what you're doing far better. We thought that creche provision was very important, that if women wanted to go then they shouldn't have the worry of what was happening to their children. We made sure there was a creche.

We've used £3,000 on the weekend schools because none of the other areas could get much money. We felt that we needed to have links with the regions so we have said at the beginnings of these meetings whoever got money would put it in the kitty because with Newcastle's applying to the Gulbenkian Foundation and the Lipman Trust and getting it, then obviously the other areas couldn't get it because it was for the same project. For Newcastle tenants we had a grant from the City: £500 for weekend schools and £500 for day schools.

Campaigning on Rents

We got people to say that they would like a rent freeze. It wasn't a strike we were going after, it was a rent freeze. We put a lot of work into it, making sure that the leaflets went out, that the leaflets were delivered. There were posters, getting the media and that and yet it was tenants that let us down.

There was also a show that could be adapted to either the full version or you could take like 20 minutes or half an hour depending on how many tenants had turned up. It was put together by "Change Gang".

We had meetings and we got information for them and they used stuff that was in the office to pull the show together. We had never been involved in play acting and that but they put it all together with information that had been gathered. They had a preview night where we could go along. We said what we thought was wrong about it. It was too long, then it was changed and then we said we felt that was alright.

Their show in itself was educational because it went right back to the first time when women started to complain about the housing. The thing in Glasgow and the fact that they'd had to stop doing decent housing because we owed the Americans money. That was actually educating tenants in a way that they'd never known. It was done in a way that it was fun.

But as I say the rents freeze didn't come off. Anyway, we got less rise than we thought we would so I suppose maybe if we hadn't have had the rents campaign that we may have got the full whack of it — the Government wanted £4. But at least they knew the tenants were sick of the rent rises.

And then we were involved in distraint. Trying to get the council to stop using it. They've now agreed to stop using distraint, so that was successful. What we did, we were working with the Law Project and West End Resources Centre and people who were interested and different social workers from different organisations — voluntary organisations through the city were all involved.

They did short case studies — not giving names — of where people had lost their furniture for a very small amount of arrears and they found they still owed the council money by the time the bailiffs got their share, which ordinary tenants don't know. What was educational in itself was that the highest amount of money goes to the people who are selling your furniture and that you can have your furniture taken off you, be left with nothing, and find out that its been sold for pennies and you still owe the council money and on top of that you've got to start replacing furniture.

So we went to talk to the Labour Party wards; we got ourselves invited there. That was education because it was something that we'd never done was actually go to a Labour Party meeting and stand there and say why you thought distraint shouldn't be used. So that was an experience in itself. We just thought it had to be done really.

What we did was we took notes that anybody could use and all you had to do was to change it to your way of speaking, you know. You have the basic information there and you could take it away and just rewrite it in a way that you would speak.

Of course Tower Blocks was still going on from the time before. We had a big meeting at the Civic Centre with the Tower Blocks campaign. We told the council that there would be about fifty or sixty and one hundred and twenty turned out. Of course they put us in the council chambers — all those posh seats and everything. And we had a right fight at the beginning of it because when I was phoning they had said that the Federation could chair it. So we were there at half past six to welcome everybody, to show everybody where they had to go and everything. And they came in about three minutes past seven, saw the crowd there and decided that I was a liar. That they hadn't agreed that we chair the meeting which was ludicrous because if they'd agreed to chair the meeting and we couldn't, first the meeting probably wouldn't have taken place and they would never have walked in three minutes late for a seven o'clock meeting. They would have been there giving everybody the soft soap and that.

What we did was we met and met and met before that big meeting and it was agreed that one person from each area of the Tower Blocks which is nine areas would stand up and say what their faults were. Even as it turned out they were the same as the other people in another area. That didn't matter. That just showed that all the blocks had the same problems. Anyway, the meeting went smashing. We hadn't said when we'd close the meeting. We thought we'd play it by ear. Then a tenant got up about bad tenants. That was when I said I thought everybody had had a fair enough say, "Can I just go over what's been promised", and closed the meeting there.

The first lot of the Tower Blocks has been done but there's still problems because Westgate Court has just been done with the storage heaters. We went up and had a look and we found out that the workmen were going to have to come back and take the storage heaters out so that they can put the insulation on! They're trying to say that it won't be a lot of expense but we think it will be because you also have the wiring which runs along the bottom above the skirting board. The skirting boards have to come off so therefore this wiring has to come off *and* the heater. We weren't happy with what they were saying so the Tenants Project paid for a consultant — a private consultant — to do a survey on the two-bedroom and the one-bedroom, and we had that information to go on. This came after that meeting when we were trying to get the district heating systems instead of the storage heating. We had this report done and we went into a meeting and they wanted a five o'clock meeting which we felt was ridiculous but we agreed. They said they had important meetings and that, that night and we said well fair enough we'll come. And then it was just going round and round. You know, they couldn't pull the report to pieces because it was a good report and I think that upset them because it was a good report. They had to admit it was a good report. And it just got to the stage when I said that I didn't think we were getting anywhere — I think we should go. So we came out into the corridors and literally we just had row after row. One officer said to me "Who are you for"? I said, "Well not for you, I'm for the tenants and there is another way that they can have it and you know it". I had a row with him about that and then we had a row with another officer. I said that you think people are daft and they're not daft.

So we're still going on and still trying to get the tenants organised. What came from the Tower Blocks campaign obviously was a lot more tenants' associations because Vale House didn't have a tenants association and they've now got one. Westgate Court didn't and they've got a very good strong one and they are actually applying now — they got two weeks free rent — but they say it isn't enough and they've actually applied to the priority teams for an extra £40 per flat for the people who have had this work done.

We're still looking at combined heat and power because Newcastle has this thing where they've committed themselves to combined heat and power and they also say that the best place to put it in is the multi-storeys and yet they're slavering on with these

Economy Sevens as a short term measure.

We've also made a video on dampness because we had a campaign up in North Kenton about damp; a week of action up there where they had a campaign in the library with damp clothing and photographs and then we decided to have street meetings to get tenants involved and from there we decided we would like a video using the North Kenton experience. It was election time for the local councillors and they used these posters saying 'cure our damp; get our vote' and the Labour fellow didn't get in because he never bothered going around. So we met the people at North Kenton to do that video, to bring out the health aspect of what it is like to live in a damp house.

So really, you're learning all the time.

CHAPTER TWO

Mary

I lived in the South of England for the first twenty-six years of my life. My two teenage sons still live there with their father. For the last nine years, I have lived in the North East with my daughter — the transition was not easy.

On the one hand a whole lot of things have happened to me, like splitting up with my husband and not knowing about social security. On the other hand, going through formal education courses like nursery nursing and secretarial, which gave me no insight or understanding into these experiences or why they happened. It was only when I got involved in tenants' action groups that I began to develop an understanding about how everything fitted into place, how we are where we are through other people's power over us.

Around 1973, I was having a really good time in my life because a secretarial course I had done enabled me to get a job that paid quite good money for the first time ever, and I had left my husband. I had freedom, money and a good job. And then my life was determined by meeting the man I moved to the North East with, because I threw myself into that relationship and after a few months I just walked out of that job to be with him. This was the sort of man on the white charger kind of stuff.

He and I actually came from quite different worlds but we at that time were living in mine, my domain kind of thing, we were living in a prosperous sort of town, we both had jobs that paid us good money and we lived together but then I became pregnant and that's where my life started to change.

At the seventh month of my pregnancy, I left and I made a clean break from the South and I came up to the North East where I had never lived before and didn't know anything about the lifestyle or anything. I was totally out of control. Suddenly my life was in their hands and I don't think I'd ever been in that situation before.

Rotten Housing

We got a flat, a council flat in Longbenton which is a huge council estate on the edge of Newcastle. I was prepared to make the best of it and I didn't have a bleak outlook but the relationship was really bad. He made me into a different person. I had never been battered before or anything, I mean although in some ways we had a good relationship, we also had a very bad one in that he was a typical North East stereotype. I feel awful saying that, I know there are men all over the country doing the same thing, but it is the Andy Capp type of person, and he turned out to be that kind of person. So anyway I had had my first taste of eleven months of being on the dole, being in a really poor situation and living in a isolated situation on a large council estate.

I was now becoming desperate about my domestic situation so I went to see a social worker. It wasn't a Social Services social worker, it was a Church of England or a North East Children's Society, I think, social worker. She came to see me at my home and she happened to know, it was pure luck, that Barnado's in the North East had recently started up a day care centre in North Kenton and were looking for a nursery nurse, staff nursery nurse. It was pure luck. I got the job which I stayed in for four years. It was a good job and that enabled me to keep my sanity and to support myself and that bloke and my child through a hell of a situation. The people I worked with understood what I was going through if I went to work with black eyes and god knows what.

There were a lot of things they didn't know about obviously, there are things you never get to tell people. I also through all this made friends with my neighbours. In fact they were more friends with me than my husband (I call him my husband) could ever have realised because they knew what a pig he was. Finally I went to the housing and through them to the social services and I went to live in a refuge, a council refuge in Wallsend because it was the only answer to getting out of that situation. I lived in the refuge for ten weeks and they rehoused me to Killingworth Towers.

I had to leave work because I lived an hour's busride away from North Kenton. I had to leave home very early in the morning with a small child and it made a very long day. I left home about 7.30 a.m. and didn't get home until 6.00 p.m. and it was becoming impossible, plus I had to think about where my daughter was to go to school. Her education was a priority and I wanted her to get into school near to where we were living so I left work.

It wasn't too bad because I had some savings and at the time you got some tax rebates and I had enough money to keep me going quite comfortably for a few months. At the same time I was lively and I was confident. I still had that energy that work gives you and I didn't want to vegetate in the house. So then I started meeting people around me, neighbours and others, which led to talking about the conditions in Killingworth, which were appalling, and the council at that point were also bringing in new measures like they put up steel barriers to stop people walking along the walkways straight along to the shops from our side of the flats. I lived on the fourth floor, perhaps I should say that, and it was murder because if you had a pram or you were an old person, or even if not, you had to go down the lift, and along and up another lift to even get to the shops. There were no lights on the staircases, the lifts didn't work. All that sort of stuff. There was rubbish everywhere because services weren't adequate for one reason or another. They cut the services of the caretakers..

Now I didn't sit down and think about that at the time. All I knew was my rubbish wasn't cleared away, I had to walk through shit on the balconies and there was always vandalism of some kind or another. Lifts stunk of urine, you name it. And everybody everywhere you went, people were talking about this. When I was working, yes people were talking about it then, but I was on the way to get the bus to work so it wasn't that bad and I knew one day that I would want to move away from it. But when you're stuck with it suddenly and you're not working, it becomes the topic of everybody's conversation.

I just began to get indignant about it all and I began to talk to this woman who lived next door to me and we said come on let's do something about it. We had the energy together to get other people together in her flat — just women who lived in our block. You know it was real energy in that room from people. We decided that we should call a public meeting. This happened straight away, you know, because everyone was saying this so everyone must agree with us. How naive we were because later on we found how difficult it was to get people to come in with you and be involved in things even though they all agree with you in passing.

I can't remember now exactly how we went about it but I remember us thinking, and this was the wrong thinking in some ways but it is the way most people who don't have that knowledge think, we must get people, important people in the community to help us. We picked the local vicar, whose church was used for virtually everything in Killingworth. He was more or less our adviser at that point. We arranged for a friend who was a photographer to take photographs of all the things we hated about the place, like the shutes where the rubbish was supposed to be, the lifts, all the vandalism and the degrading things that you can imagine we took photographs of and this guy got them done at a really cheap rate. We paid for them ourselves. We put them on posters. My whole life was taken over by doing this. I was eating, sleeping and breathing it and really enthusiastic about it. It changed my life. The big thing was moving towards this public meeting and it took us three weeks to do this. Honestly what a nightmare, if somebody told me to do this in three weeks now and I have done the training, I would freak out. I wouldn't do it.

Anyway we thought we had to get all "the important people" there. What we really needed to do was just to get the tenants there. You know, I mean, because those "important" people were really the people who would keep us down. We thought, great, they're listening to us. Of course they were listening to us, because we posed a threat to them didn't we? Now the councillors were frightened and the housing were frightened and honestly it was really murder trying to get them on the telephone.

Three hundred people turned up to this meeting. Three hundred people for a meeting! The meeting really gave us an understanding of where we stood in relation to the tenants and in relation to the establishment. It was interesting that all the "important" people were all sat together on the front line and the others were all sat at the back. The local M.P. gave his political speech (you know the way they are) so practised and polished that it kind of took the wind out of everyone's sails.

I had never had anything to do with working class action at all. I didn't think of it in those terms at all. I was just a person who was living there and leading something.

Involvement with the North East Tenants' Organisation

We had a coffee morning and we had a raffle to raise money because we knew we were going to need money for postage and to do all the things. We were already getting on the right tracks by ourselves actually but obviously we didn't know anything about local government and all that kind of stuff. I think we would have got there by ourselves but probably along different tracks and probably we would have ended up eating out of their hands moreso. However NETO gave us some guidelines and worked with us to an extent but we actually did all the things ourselves. You know, they just told us the best way of going about things. We ended up with a committee of tenants. These twelve people were really, really good. We gave ourselves roles within our group. I was amazed when I think back at what we did knowing how little knowledge most of us had on how to organise all those things.

Now when I say with NETO's help, we knew what we wanted. What they helped us with more were the physical things like where to sit the councillors and how to be positive in the meeting and not let them get one over on you kind of stuff, and this meeting I'll never forget ever because I think it was one of the most successful things we have ever done. It was real tactical stuff. They tried their old tricks about calling you by your first name and talking about all their committees and all that and trying to blind you with science. You know the council stuff. Of course, we knew what they were going to do. And then, you see, they started to be heavy and they started not to like us because they realised we really meant business and I had one of the councillors ringing me up at one point because we were handing out press reports and doing all these things to freak up the council and the housing. I remember one of the councillors ringing me up one day and telling me off because I had told the press about something that had happened at a meeting between us.

Really you needed a house that everybody could use and integrate and that is what happened finally after a lot of fighting. And then the tenants had a place that they could use to talk about issues that affected everybody and that is what we were working towards.

Wider Campaigns

Now during that time NETO came along and started to talk a little bit more about other things they were involved in and asked us if we would like to go to meetings and if we would like to use their equipment at the Resource Centre. I remember us going back and saying what a run down place the resource centre was and what a terrible building it was and everything. Not realising that all people who are fighting these campaigns all had to work under these pressures and they were usually given poor conditions to work from.

It was only when you went to a central meeting that you would hear about other people's actions and realise how it related to national issues and to politics. We had to start really by thinking about the government and what government was doing. Obviously you had to hammer away at your own politicians but you really needed to join in with the greater scheme of things and that's how things began to happen. We went to a couple of day schools, but it became I was the only person that was available. Everyone in a tenants' group is always under such pressure really, you know, i.e. if you are in a tenants' group, you're fighting in the first place about the conditions you are living in or something, and it's really difficult to be involved in other things outside of that. And for women it's difficult because most of them have got men that don't want them, that feel a bit jealous about them becoming involved in things. Anyway perhaps I should go back a bit and say that that man came back into my life, and then became heavy. Cutting a long story short, I used to turn up at meetings with bruises and cuts and things and used to give feeble excuses for why I had them. Now that wasn't only happening to me. I mean that happens to a lot of people in different ways. Like the dinner on the table syndrome.

I began to talk to one of the women involved in NETO about Women's Aid which I didn't really know about even though I had been in a refuge (which was not a Women's Aid Refuge). We began to talk about other issues like how difficult it is for women to fight these things and that opened up that whole group thing. I mean there are difficulties: often women can't get to groups because of men's jealousy and antagonism. Women are meant to be at home, not putting the world to rights in some way.

Moving out of Killingworth

A lot of us were moved out. I mean I think I'm talking more or less about moving away from the tenants' group bit because I moved on to other things and a lot of us, not overnight, but gradually, and during quite a short period of time, began to be moved out. Now I had to move out anyway because of the violence but most other people were moved out very quickly. Some people who had been waiting for years suddenly got decent houses where they wanted them and in the period of time in which I was involved (which was only really a period of a few months that we were really heavily involved) four people — four people got moved.

So from there, I was still involved with NETO and I'd been to a few day schools and they were also planning to have weekend schools which was absolutely fantastic because I didn't have any money. I was in a bit of a rut anyway and I was keen to learn more about those sorts of things, all these issues. And this really gave me an opportunity to get away. To get away from all my problems, to get away from where I was living with my child as well. I mean I didn't have to worry about anybody looking after her. I could go away and be fed and have somewhere to sleep and someone would entertain my child at the same time. You know, despite all the things about learning, just those things in themselves were brilliant — brilliant for tenants to be able to do that.

It was a series of day schools — four linked weekends on the history of council housing. Three lots of groups came, one from

Sheffield, one from Coventry and one from the North East. Things that stay with me were, they used theatre groups and it was the first time I'd ever seen theatre groups used to educate people about their own living conditions in educationals, their own situations and it was extremely interesting. There was no way that any of the discussions, anything that we were reading could have compared with what was illustrated by the theatre group. You know, it just put it all together in one hour. Teaching people, putting things together and teaching people something. Other things that were done were role plays (situations which one doesn't normally do) which again for me was the best way of learning because it takes me a long time to wade through papers and to put things together. And they were talking about the market system. The role play was about the market system and how it works and it was brilliant. I don't think to this day I would understand it if it hadn't been for that particular role play.

Women's Politics: Women's Aid

During this time I'd gone to live in a house where there were two women who were very much involved in different kinds of political activity and women's action and I began to learn about feminism which I really didn't know very much about before. I mean, I really didn't know it was going on around me all the time through ordinary women's action whether it be through a trade union or through a theatre group or through a tenants' group or whatever. I didn't really see that this community action was really education for people. The things that they were involved in were working against the things that destroy most women. Not only male violence, there are a lot of other things in society. Like attitudes of people generally. There were lots of different journals in the house and a lot of books. I found, in the beginning, this literature quite distressing and didn't understand how they could read it all the time. It began to get me down until gradually you know, a lot of women went to the house all the time for different reasons, and I began to listen to them talking and they invited me to go to things with them like, you know, a group that was maybe meeting somewhere. They did it, I think, for me to socialise with people but through that kind of socialising I learnt about a lot of different women's issues. To become involved in that helps you to think constructively about how you might participate through your own learning and through your new understanding in helping to change what's going on. Not necessarily politically but I do think a lot of these things are political issues, you can't get away from that.

A lot of women, the majority of women don't get involved in

politics because it seems frightening and it's sort of male orientated and it's depressing and all those things that I said beforehand. Then gradually you begin to see how together you might do things, talking to women about their ideas and feelings and working out whole new perspectives. And not feeling depressed about it. Not feeling so threatened by it. Feeling more positive which is important. It's the same as the tenants thing, it's the same as anybody taking any kind of action. You've actually got to feel positive about it. It's not something that somebody else can make you do, it's got to come from yourself.

A friend introduced me to the local group of Women's Aid and because of my experiences I got involved in the group too. And I found that I had as much to say, if not more, than some of those women who were quite middle class. I didn't have to sit quietly because I knew as much as they did through my own life experiences. Suddenly you didn't feel as threatened as you might do if you go to a group — a formal education group.

It was great anyway and also people all participate. You know if somebody needs to approach the council or the press or take some kind of action. You're not looking in from the outside, you're part of it. Every step we made, everything we did was learning something new really. Then I got to know more and more and I got to go to conferences and other meetings further afield.

Then I heard that the worker at Women's Aid in Sunderland was leaving which meant that there was only one worker at Women's Aid and the group had got to know me by this time and somebody said would I like a temporary job at Women's Aid? Did I think I could cope with it? So I went down to the refuge there and talked to the women who were living there and some of the voluntary helpers and I went for an informal interview and they gave me the job. So I worked there for ten weeks with the other worker which was very useful.

By this time it was the Spring of 1980.

The Sunderland Youth and Community Work Course

Perhaps I should just say that prior to doing this I had met a tutor on the Sunderland Youth and Community Work Course who suggested that I did the course because it would allow me to have a wider range of experiences and he felt that, you know, academically it didn't matter if I had GCE's or degrees or anything else. Coming from him, him being the tutor and suggesting that I did it, gave me confidence into thinking that I could do it. He really gave me confidence to apply to do the course. The reason why I wanted to do it was because I had a lot of knowledge now that I felt I could use in a job but I had no qualification to go and do that kind of job. So that was my main motivation — to get the qualification. Plus I also was hungry for knowledge, to deepen and widen this new found knowledge I had.

The Interview

I think it was sometime during the summer I went for the formal interview which was really frightening. I had one tutor (not the one who had invited me to apply) and two students and the tutor diminished me completely. He made me feel like a quivering jelly and I never thought that I would get on the course. They wanted to know if we could actually string words together and put them down on paper so we had a brief verbal introduction to people and then we had to write about poverty and we had to write this thing about relative and absolute poverty which was absolute bullshit.

After all that, you go in for the formal slaughter — the interview. And the tutor asked me this and I can't remember it word for word but it was 'What did I think about the society we live in'? You know!!!! I was gob-struck. I thought Christ I've got to be intelligent here. When I first went in I felt sort of confident because I'd heard how this course was supposed to be so supportive and orientated to people. But with that question I felt smashed because I thought shit, what am I going to say? I didn't have any jargon. I found out later in the course that you can actually get away with things by using jargon which I don't like and I'm not happy about. Anyone can use jargon. You don't have to understand it. And I did have an understanding about what he was talking about but I couldn't use the kind of words he wanted or what I felt he wanted. But, anyway, I got on the course.

Suddenly I was thrown back in to being with men again. Now this might sound really stupid, but I remember feeling so intimidated in the group, really nervous, sort of shaking inside even and I couldn't work out why and it was during talking in these small groups that I did realise to a point why it was — it was that I was put back into a position where I was working with men again. I'd been used to being in groups with women where you can just plunge in, you don't feel self-conscious or any of that kind of threatening stuff that goes on unconsciously but I was then conscious of it, you see and I had to relearn working closely with men again. So therefore, when I first went on, for the first term at least, I felt very intimidated. I really got angry with myself afterwards at not being able to speak in the group, in a discussion group. I couldn't speak and I felt that I was letting myself down and him down and I shouldn't be on the course and I almost felt that I'd made a mistake. This all began to change when we went away from the college. We were broken up into small groups. Six of us went to a project in South Shields and we had to do a profile of an area called Laygate in South Shields which was extremely interesting.

It gave you an opportunity to look at things you were interested in and to develop them in your own way and work with somebody else on that and because that person wasn't a tutor you were able, you know, to use skills that we hadn't used for a long time. I mean I started typing again, I went to meetings in the evening and we took notes and all these old things that we'd never done from school maybe, we did together again. We had to discipline ourselves and all the time there were new things and there were new challenges.

It was by then another term and we were going into our first placement. I chose media because in everything I'd done, you needed the media. I felt that any area of community work that I was going to go into, and I didn't know what I wanted to go into, I would need knowledge of how to use the media. How to draft newsletters, how to do layout, to learn certain skills, to use the media.

One thing I did find out was the way I can work. I found out a lot about myself in that I always think of myself as a lazy person because I will never willingly take on responsibilities that I don't really have to but I think I can honestly say that I really work hard when I have to because I gave myself some kind of motivation. Perhaps that was a good thing about the course, that I had to produce something at the end of the day that was worthwhile and I didn't feel that I could sham. I think that will determine the kind of job I get as well, you know, I can't take something just because it's a community work job. That's given me a knowledge about myself. I'm saying this to myself I think because basically I put myself down all the time but in those two things I really did work really hard in a way that I never thought I could.

My reason for choosing adult education as a second placement was the type of group I would be working with. I didn't want to be working with a voluntary set up because I learnt that it really has a lot of headaches which I didn't want. Also, my tutor wanted me to go to an agency where I would have an opportunity to look at more than one aspect of community work. Adult Education was different. I'd worked with children and I'd worked with mothers in that situation when I worked as a nursery nurse and yes I'd worked on the media which involved interviewing people who worked in the community and adult education is about all those things. I gained from that placement in many ways. I gained in terms of skills and knowledge of the different kinds of community work, i.e. looking at education in the community, informal education.

I had never really stopped to think about education as anything other than school and college or university or whatever formal channels even though I had some informal education. I had looked on it as probably something else. I hadn't sat down to evaluate that before.

You really have to start at the beginning and talk about people meeting together and from meeting together in a group, people learn things. They talk about the sort of things that they want to talk about, the things that are important to them, the things that affect their lives in the setting that they may be living in, and, wherever they may be come from, to those particular groups they are all working class women. Some may be in better financial positions than others. Some may have better education or a different kind of upbringing or whatever. General differences all over but from one part of the country to another, working class women with children, especially ones who are at home, mostly mothers who are at home, have that thing in common that they are at home with their children. They need to talk to other women and the other differences, i.e. financial, education or what have you, are really quite irrelevant because they will come together.

Looking back on it I think that again one has to go through, you have to go through, you have to make mistakes and you have to blunder, you have to go through it. You say the wrong things and you say, "god what do they think of me" and all that kind of stuff but really its good, you've got to do it and push it. Push yourself right through because if I did it again now, I would be able to do it better than I did then. I've learnt by now from all the things I've told you a lot about community work and I feel really that I am the community worker now, you know. That I'm in advance of those women in the group in terms of, not in terms of intelligence, not superior to them academically in any sense in any way at all as a mother or anything else, but that I have learnt a lot of community things and that I have met a lot of community people and that I've got a lot of information. I've now got a whole kind of library in my own head of community arts or local history or computers. I know people who could do it and I know the people who could do it without being formal. You know, the people who could do it in a relaxed comfortable way.

The Health Educationals

I'm working part-time at the moment helping plan this series of health educationals. It's something I haven't done before. I haven't helped to organise dayschools. I've been to dayschool but I hadn't helped to organise them. I hadn't done much coordinating. From my point of view, I think it is an exciting opportunity to be done in Newcastle because it hasn't been, to my knowledge, nobody has organised a series of dayschools on these issues for women before, so it is something new. You know, it's a launching pad, it's a taster, it's a chance, it's an opportunity for them to possibly start off something from all those things for themselves in their own areas, join something or raise issues that haven't been, in fact, raised at all. We're going to learn, the people who organise are going to learn from it and as workers they will benefit from it. The people who are really working in health projects — the three main health projects in Newcastle — should benefit from it immensely because, hopefully, they will take back with them a whole wealth of information to use with the women in their areas. To create, perhaps organise further dayschools, to start off groups, to write something. That's what I hope.

Present Status

At least I have some choice about my future. I have got a degree of control now of my life. Probably for the first time ever I suppose. It's not simply a case of having a qualification, it's through a different kind of learning experience. I'd analysed things before but in a kind of negative way and now I do it in a more positive way and I am more assertive in my own mind about ideas and actions. It's an overall thing. It's not just I've suddenly woken up and I'm alright today kind of thing. I think it's going through the course and learning how to analyse, evaluate. It was not the college — I emphasise that it was not the college — it was my placements in the community and it was the opportunity that was created through that course. Nobody would have given me that responsibility. It sometimes is a pity for people who are doing voluntary community work because they have just as much knowledge, they know what they're doing. You know, they're not really credited with anything.

People see me as a real person. I've got that qualification and here I am, that's where it's brought me to. I feel actually, although I can work in an unpaid way, that I need to work and I've got a lot of skills and why shouldn't I be paid for them because I see a lot of people being paid a lot of money for community work that I can do and why should I do it for nothing? Why shouldn't I get paid for it? You know all these voluntary agencies that are set up are sometimes really being ripped off because those women, and it's mainly women that are doing it, are doing very valuable jobs and if it is somebody who has been trained and qualified and bringing things together they should be paid properly to do a proper job. If it's the voluntary agency that's set up and it benefits people, then it should be made into a real job.

PART II

First Time Round

CHAPTER THREE

From Raising Awareness To Positive Action: Opportunities For Intervention

Val Millman

Personal Experience

In 1975, the year in which the Sex Discrimination Act was passed, a group of staff at the Community College I was teaching in organised a seminar entitled 'Education of the Female'. All the teaching staff were expected to attend and participate in a discussion of academic and pastoral issues.

A working party was set up to investigate girls' experiences of particular areas of school life and, in subsequent years (by which time the working party thankfully had been renamed 'The Education of Women and Girls') a variety of strategies were adopted to try to raise the awareness of colleagues and to improve the quality of education received by girls in the college.

In retrospect I can now see that we were working in considerable isolation, and that the strategy we adopted demanded more radical changes in people's attitudes than was possible at the time. The majority of teachers were still unaware that the new law had significant implications for educational institutions. It was only in the late 70's that research on sex differentiation in schools began to filter through to educationalists and government reports began to highlight sex inequality in the curriculum. In the earlier vacuum of the mid 70's our own attempts to take positive action on behalf of the girls had been seen either as subversive or as fanatical so that, over a period of years, support for the working party dwindled and we failed to effect changes in the mainstream curriculum on the scale that was necessary to improve girls' experience of school.

Times Have Changed

In 1981 I was appointed to the Schools Council to set up an Equal

Opportunities in Education Centre and a year later, to take over as National Co-ordinator of the Sex Differentiation Project. After six years of school involvement in what had been seen by many as 'a subversive or fanatical activity', it was quite a contrast to be paid by a prestigious government body to promote the same activities in Local Education Authorities. Indeed, by the early 1980s the Sex Discrimination Act had caught up with a number of LEAs and educationalists throughout the country were beginning to realise that sex differentiation was a mainstream educational issue which could no longer be ignored.

As we move into the mid 80's struggling to maintain high educational standards in the face of economic cutbacks, the issue of equal opportunities is, perhaps surprisingly, continuing to make its mark on educational agendas up and down the country. In November 1983, Sir Keith Joseph claimed that 'the education girls receive is inadequate — they are entitled to expect better', endorsing the legitimate professional concern increasingly expressed by teachers at all levels of education. Given the majority of women in teaching it seems unlikely that this concern will disappear. Certainly it will be a struggle in coming years to obtain sufficient resources for radical and unrestrained curricular innovation. But there will be many opportunities for positive intervention, some of which will be identified in the remainder of the chapter, most of which will be more effective if teachers work closely with colleagues outside schools. In the current climate teachers cannot afford to sink back into the traditional insularity of schools. They need to explore broad based strategies for achieving sex equality in schools focusing on some of the following questions which are fundamental to everyone working with girls.

Current Questions

— Should we help girls to value their traditional interests, or encourage their activities into male dominated areas, or both?
— Should we work with girls in mixed or single sex groups? Should positive action strategies involve men or be women-only initiatives?
— Is it enough to talk about being non-sexist and working towards equal opportunities, or do we want an anti-sexist positive discrimination strategy?

Sex Differentiation: The Problem

'You can't plan your future. In any case, girls can't go anywhere because they're not as clever as boys.'
A sixteen year old Midlands girl. (Millman, Coventry LEA 1982)

This girl's inability to 'go anywhere' bears as little relation to her lack of intelligence as her brother's inability to make his mother a cup of tea. But she has learnt to blame herself rather than the limited opportunities open to her. Success in public life, primarily a male domain, is considered to depend on intelligence and is rewarded by financial gain and status. But for those who work within the home there are no such rewards — they therefore feel unable to 'go anywhere' in their lives.

It is predominantly women whose life-chances are restricted in this way. From earliest childhood society sets aside for them 'feminine' corners of experience. Young girls enthusiastically shape themselves into their 'feminine' roles mirroring the behaviour of women with whom they have most frequent contact. Boys too practise being 'masculine'. By the age of three, both sexes understand the sex-appropriate behaviour expected of them and as they grow older they become increasingly reluctant to step outside these boundaries. On entering school, traditional boundaries become sharply defined. As each sex develops a different set of expectations and behaviour, boys learn to grasp a greater degree of control over their lives than girls.

In The Primary School:
Demarcation of Male and Female Territory

To the casual observer, the caring parent and even the seasoned professional, girls and boys appear to play happily together in the nursery and infant classrooms. They move freely from area to area, sometimes on their own, sometimes working in pairs or groups. They play together, talk together and learn together. It is hard to believe that their behaviour is being shaped by notions of adulthood and future.

Recent research contradicts first impressions. Despite teachers' intentions to provide both sexes with the same learning opportunities, girls and boys devise for themselves a sexually differentiated curriculum. This is particularly apparent in 'free activity' periods when girls and boys spend a greater proportion of their time playing sex-appropriate games and activities (Kohlberg 1966). Although younger children are willing to experiment with cross-sex toys, (eg. boys with dolls and girls with trains), they are usually quick to abandon these under pressure from their peers (Serbin 1978). This pressure becomes stronger as children grow older; an initial awareness of sex differences leads to a demarcation of male and female territories — boys take over the fort while girls defend the Wendy House!

In a recent survey of classroom behaviour in a hundred nursery and infant schools in Manchester, teachers observed that children's activity choices became increasingly stereotyped between the ages of three and six:

Activity	Age Group 3-5 (Nursery) % Boys	% Girls	Age Group 5 & Over (Infant) % Boys	% Girls
Wendy House/Home	42	58	down 34	66
Corner/Dolls House	46	54	22	up 78
Constructional play	64	36	66	down 34
Bricks, cars, trains	69	31	up 73	27

Note:
'Feminine' activity: *Fewer* boys and *More* girls participate in older age group.

'Masculine' activity: *More* boys but *fewer* girls participate in older age group.

On occasions when girls and boys did play in non-traditional areas of the room, close observation revealed sex differences in the ways they approached activities. Boys tended to play in gangs more than the girls, adopting a more aggressive role. For example, three or four boys will make a raid on a Wendy House and threaten those playing there! (see Whyte 1983).

Developing a 'Feminine' Approach to Learning

The use of a video-film to analyse the behaviour of girls and boys in the classroom has enabled teachers and researchers to identify differences, not just in interests of girls and boys and in their approaches to play, but differences in their styles of learning. Boys appear to be more task-oriented while girls appear to be more teacher-oriented. Girls try to gain teachers' approval by passively conforming to rules and norms, while boys actively define their own space. It is the boys who dominate the activities taking place in the classroom, the playground and on the sportsfield. At primary level these differences seem to result in girls being more successful. From the earliest age at which children's intellectual performance can be measured, girls score higher on all kinds of achievement tests (except visual spatial) up to the age of eleven. They learn to speak, read and count at earlier ages than boys and maintain their overall headstart well into their first year at secondary school.

Indeed, it has been common practice for many years to lower the boys' eleven plus exam pass level to ensure that equal numbers of girls and boys obtained grammar school places — this form of positive discrimination towards boys has been necessary to raise their level of achievement in certain areas of schooling. Girls' mean reading scores are marginally higher than boys at the age of eleven and they hold more positive attitudes to reading (APU 1981). In view of this, most schools have prioritised remedial reading classes to enable the boys to catch up. Today, in spite of research that shows that practical training can improve girls' spatial scores (Connor, Shackman and Serbin 1978) specific teaching classes for spatial ability are virtually unknown in the primary school.

Boys succeed in retaining a greater level of self-confidence than girls even in areas where girls perform better. Boys for example show greater confidence in their mathematical ability. In recent surveys of mathematical performance at eleven, significantly more boys than girls believed that they usually understand a mathematical idea quickly, that they were usually correct in their work and that maths was one of their better subjects (APU). Girls, in contrast, reacted more negatively to failure, believing it to be caused by their own lack of ability rather than lack of effort or some external circumstances. By this stage of schooling, girls appear to be bringing to their academic work, attitudes and expectations which restrict rather than enhance their approaches to learning. Relative to boys, girls' overall pattern of achievement deteriorates rapidly in the early years of secondary school. This deterioration in girls' overall achievement is marked by an increasing loss of interest in certain subject areas. In secondary schools girls tend, for example, to avoid choosing to take mathematical and scientific subjects at exam level. While it is likely that the secondary curriculum is partially responsible for this, it is insufficient on its own to account for a marked down-turn in certain subject areas only, and particularly those in which girls have been previously successful. It seems likely that we have to look deeper than this for causes, beneath the school's formal curriculum to the sexually differentiated expectations and aspirations that begin to take shape in the primary classroom.

The Effect of the 'Hidden Curriculum'

Current research findings lay much of the blame on the 'hidden curriculum' which children experience at all levels of schooling. While it is true that some primary schools separate girls and boys for P.E. and Craft activities, children spend most of their time studying topics in mixed groupings. Yet, by the age of eleven, irrespective of their attainment, girls and boys have developed sexually differentiated attitudes towards different subject areas. Children as young as eight have been shown to perceive science as a 'masculine' subject (Harvey 1980). Mischel (1967) observed that boys who refuse to sew a doll's dress in needlework are happy sewing the hem of a tent at scout camp. Ten year olds can obtain different scores on parts of a test according to whether they are 'being themselves' or 'pretending' to be a member of the opposite sex! (Hargreaves 1977). This pattern re-emerges at subject choice time in the secondary school; girls and boys say that they would choose a different range of options if they were members of the opposite sex (Schools Council 1982). Gender clearly asserts a powerful influence and is a key factor in determining individual interest and choice. Many teachers limit their pupils' choices in life by unconsciously reinforcing gender stereotypes through the organisation and ethos of their classroom. Children learn as much through their school's 'hidden curriculum' as they do through the planned classroom activities.

Making 'Choices'

Faced with a choice of subjects or activities, children usually opt for areas in which they have interest and confidence; often these are areas with which they are already familiar, and invariably they are in line with traditional sex-stereotypes. Adult expectations shape these stereotyped choices from a young age. Parents give approval to their children for 'choosing' sex-appropriate games and toys. Teachers encourage the segregation and polarisation of the sexes in the same way. In large classes where there is limited time in which to get to know pupils' individual characteristics, teachers often base their expectations on gender. Chasen (1975) showed that teachers of young children assume that girls are 'better behaved, play more often in the Wendy House and clean up more readily' while boys 'play with bricks and have greater physical strength'. Frequently such assumptions are contradicted by reality — the 'two strong fourth year lads' who are asked to move the dining tables are often smaller and slighter in build than their female contemporaries! But the myths are perpetuated and boys are complimented on their strength while girls are praised for their appearance.

Most teachers set different behavioural standards for girls and boys, which can be seen clearly through the sanctions that are applied in the classroom. Boys are allowed to be noisier and rougher while girls are reproached for behaving in 'an unladylike fashion'. Teachers tell girls that they must not get dirty, and, if they do get dirty, to wash. Boys are told to wash but not to avoid the dirt (Hodgeon 1983). These differences, while apparently trivial, can have important educational consequences for girls. Not only are teachers disapproving of certain types of activity, but they are also encouraging a passive conforming approach to life and to learning. Later girls will be disadvantaged by their lack of initiative and fear of problem solving. Behavioural expectations and educational achievement are therefore closely linked. Girls are less likely to succeed in 'masculine' subjects if their teachers and friends consider them 'odd' for choosing them. They are less likely to develop academic self confidence if their interests and activities are devalued or taken less seriously by teachers. When a boy is punished by being asked to play in a corner occupied by the girls, or is called sissy for wanting to play with dolls, the girls learn to see themselves in a negative light. When topic work is repeatedly based on boys' interests (to prevent the boys from becoming disruptive) the girls can only conclude that they are of secondary importance. When boys gain 75% of the teacher's attention the girls see that they take second place (Spender 1982). Despite boys' poorer achievement in the primary school, teachers frequently believe that they have greater potential than girls and go to great lengths to capture their interest and develop potential. Where boys fail they are often described as 'lacking motivation'; where girls fail they are more often described as 'lacking ability'.

The Effect of School Organisation

Beyond the classroom, segregation of the sexes is further sanctioned by the ethos and organisation of the school itself. Girls and boys use separate lavatories, separate cloakrooms and sometimes separate playgrounds. They line up separately outside the classrooms and sit separately in assemblies; their names are called out separately on the registers. Forms of organisation which are claimed to be of merely administrative convenience to staff are responsible for teaching children that gender provides the framework within which much of their daily experience will be determined. Girls learn that to be female is not only to be separate from boys, but often to take second place on the register, in the dinner queue and on the periphery of the playground. As they grow older they are continually reminded of their marginal status through the images of women they see in books and on television. It should not surprise us to hear of the ten year old girl who insisted to her teacher that 'only boys can be doctors' despite the fact that her mother was a GP! Sex-stereotyping is a powerful and persistent influence on young people throughout their daily lives at school.

In the Secondary School

In a longitudinal study of about 5000 children born in 1946, girls who had been doing better than their male counterparts at the end of their primary schooling scored lower on all tests (except verbal intelligence) than the boys at the age of fifteen. The boys obtained more 'O' levels and 'A' levels, and, regardless of school leaving qualifications, were more likely to receive further education or training (Douglas and Cherry 1977). The position has slightly improved in recent years. The overall participation rate at 'O' level and 'A' level is higher for girls than boys but about a fifth more boys than girls take three or more 'A' levels; this is reflected in the different entry rates to higher education. But sometimes it is useful to consider exam entries, achievement levels and subject choices as separate indices of educational equality, for there is sharp segregation in exam subjects taken by girls and boys. Girls are gaining qualifications in areas which are now less valuable as 'passports' into higher education or as 'exchange tokens' in the job market:

> 'In the fourth and fifth years approximately four times as many boys as girls take 'O' level and CSE physics, and twice as many take chemistry. Fewer girls than boys attempt 'O' level maths, and a smaller proportion achieve high grades. Beyond the age of sixteen the under-representation of girls in the physical sciences and maths and the employment opportunities these can lead to, becomes progressively more obvious. In computer studies at 'O' and 'A' level, despite the apparent association between the subject and forces of change in modern society, boys outnumber girls by two to one and there is little evidence that the balance is altering. In traditional craft subjects girls and boys are even more clearly separated. In 1980, forty times as many boys as girls took CSE woodwork, and a hundred times as many took metalwork. Twenty-six times as many took CSE technical drawing. At 'O' level the differences in these subjects were greater still.'
>
> (*Orr 1982*)

Many people believed that the post-war shift towards co-educational schooling would provide both sexes with the opportunity to study a wider range of subjects than had previously been available in single sex schools. Unfortunately sex-stereotyped attitudes of parents, teachers and pupils have prevented the majority of young people from grasping this opportunity. In some cases co-education appears to have narrowed rather than broadened educational opportunity. Although the most recent research suggests that there is no significant difference in overall achievement levels between girls who attend mixed or single sex schools, there *is* a difference in the subjects they choose and in the way they approach classroom learning. Although there is a proportion of girls' schools that is still flouting the requirements of the Sex Discrimination Act (1975) by failing to provide craft, design and technology facilities for girls (GATE 1983), girls in single sex schools are still more likely to choose traditionally masculine subjects such as physics, maths and technology (HMI 1977).

Co-educational Opportunities

Mixed schools seem to polarise girls' and boys' subject choices. In girls-only schools women are more likely to teach the whole range of subjects and occupy senior positions in the school's management hierarchy. In this environment, girls can not only be less preoccupied with gaining approval from the opposite sex but they can also base their choices and aspirations on a wider range of adult role models than is available in a mixed school.

Dale Spender (1982) has shown that boys dominate mixed groups, demanding and gaining a disproportionate share of teacher attention and classroom resources. Girls in single sex classes do not have to compete for the teacher's help; they have been shown to display more confidence and a greater willingness to ask and answer questions.

In a recent study of co-educational 'A' level classes (1982) Michelle Stanworth found that both men and women teachers took more interest in male pupils, asking them more questions in class and giving them more help. The same teachers underestimated girls' ability and ambitions. One girl who was getting top marks in both her main 'A' level subjects and who wanted a career in the Diplomatic Service was described by her woman teacher as 'likely to become the personal assistant to somebody rather important'. In this study, the teacher's attitudes and expectations were echoed by the pupils. One boy said:

> 'I can't really imagine where the girls will end up. You can't really imagine they want to *be* anything whereas the boys, they definitely want to get to university and get good jobs.'

Contrary to the boys' impressions, the majority of girls and young women *are* ambitious to 'achieve something in their lives' but they have been encouraged by both parents and teachers, not to mention society at large, to define achievement in different ways. As girls move towards adulthood, they have to develop 'double vision' — a view of the future where personal achievement will be largely determined by commitments to husband and children. Most girls and young women find it impossible to envisage the pattern of their futures, to define their hopes and aspirations in concrete terms. They believe that they will have to put others' needs and interests before their own and it is this expectation of future priorities that has determined so much of their educational experience (Millman 1982).

Future Roles as Wives and Mothers

Girls' interest in, and choice of, school subjects is therefore directly related to the subject matter's potential use in the future. In a recent comparison of girls and boys who had just completed a 3rd year technology course, it was found that all of the boys but none of the girls thought that 'the course work would be useful to them in their future lives, both in employment and outside'. This expectation had motivated the boys but 'switched off' the girls (Millman 1984). Girls will therefore continue to choose to study office work, childcare and home economics as long as they believe that these subjects will lead them to jobs which closely fit in with their future roles as wives and mothers.

In choosing these subjects, girls are also opting to learn in an environment free from the conflict posed by the boys in the mixed classroom. In the childcare class there is likely to be a concensus of purpose, a uniformity of approach which provides girls with learning conditions not available to them in computer studies. Here, the subject matter, the classroom ethos, the access to machines will be determined by the boys' needs. Not only is it likely that the teacher will pay more attention to the boys in the class, but also that lesson content will be geared to boys' experiences and interests. In a school where for every parent who buys a daughter a computer there are thirteen parents who buy one for their sons (TES 1983), what chance do the girls stand of taking a lead in using the computer?

Research confirms that the performance of one sex or the other can vary according to the 'maleness' or 'femaleness' of topics set over a wide range of subject areas. A study of science and mathematics syllabuses suggests that examples tend to be related to traditionally male interests and activities. Bob Wood (1976) found in his analysis of GCE 'O' level maths attainment that the same problem, set in a different context, could produce significant sex differences in performance. Although, in mathematical terms, the concept was identical, he found that there was a marked disparity when the problem was set in a male context; females found the problem harder to solve. Lesley Kant (1982) also points out that the language of textbooks and examination papers tends to assume that examinees are always male, with constant references to 'he', 'him' and 'man'. Research confirms that the constant use of words closely associated with maleness seriously undermines female interest, involvement and achievement. A continual string of sex-stereotyped messages runs through the 'hidden curriculum' of both primary and secondary schools. Girls in single sex schools do not necessarily gain a broader education by escaping the male-dominated resources and classrooms of the mixed schools. It may be that opportunities offered to them are restricted by teachers' stereotypical views of their inevitable future roles as wives and mothers. As Ann Bone concludes in her report on single sex schooling:

> 'It does not make much difference which type of school girls go to, both are failing to ensure that they get the same education as boys.'
> (*Observer 1983*)

At sixteen girls emerge from their school fifth year classes with a less confident, less independent world-view than boys and a set of qualifications which only equips them for a narrow, low paid, fast disappearing corner of the labour market. If they succeed in finding paid work they will have fewer promotion prospects than boys and find it four times harder than boys to obtain release from their employers for further training. If they find themselves unemployed they may either stay at home, helping mothers and sisters with domestic chores or they may decide motherhood is their only hope of adult status and become single parents. Or they may go onto a Youth Training Scheme which will continue to train them in obsolete typing and clerical skills, preparing them for jobs which will shortly no longer exist.

At sixteen, the *Future* seems a long way off, with *Marriage* and *Motherhood* coming in between. It is often not until ten years later that women realise how deeply the education system failed them, how it did not prepare them for the lives they would be leading. As one woman said,

> 'It's been too long. I would have to start all over again. I wish the teachers had pushed me harder — I didn't really bother to think about my third year subjects, just choosing the same as my friends. I'll make sure my daughter continues her studies. I'll make sure she has a better life than mine.'

A television programme reported another woman's experience:

> 'S had no idea what sort of job she wanted to do right through to the end of her 6th year when she left school. She said that no one helped her looking for a job in her last year at school.
> She had not been on a work experience course in her 4th year but now wished that she had. She said, "A lot of our girls end up in factories so the school should let them see what those places are like earlier on."

S had excellent exam qualifications — English, Physics, Biology 'O' levels, CSE 1 Maths (although she found maths the most difficult subject at school) and CSE 1 Social Studies. Three years after leaving school she realised that she would like to do laboratory work at some point in the future. There were all girls in the family and S's father had "always encouraged them to find out about things and understand why things work in a certain way."

At the time of interview S was on maternity leave from her post as clerical officer with the GPO. She had become pregnant through contraceptive failure and thought that she would like to return to work when her maternity leave was over. She expected to be having another baby in three years time.

S had been on a 3-month clerical course for unemployed school leavers shortly after leaving school. She had thought of a mechanic's course to use her sciences but was put off because people would think 'it's odd'. She then started a work experience placement at Chrysler testing car parts which she enjoyed very much because she was finding out things. But then she saw a permanent clerical job advertised at the GPO which she applied for. She had been on a four-week training course here, had been promoted at work and had joined a union.'

Double Vision 1982

'S' had lived in the same area of the City throughout her life, only moving up the road from her parents when she got married at eighteen. Not only had her family, especially her father, had a strong influence on her development, but also the organisations and institutions to whom she had turned at different points in her life. 'S' had always been shocked by the lack of contact that existed between organisations working at such close quarters in the local community — the schools, the youth and careers service, the housing department and health services, training agencies, employers and the union which she had joined.*

Equal Opportunities: An Educational Issue

Despite a move towards Community Education in some parts of the country, schools have been traditionally jealous of their territory, sometimes issuing stark reminders of this to the local community by putting noticeboards in school playgrounds saying 'Parents are not permitted beyond this point'. Similarly, schools have often been slow to respond to changes demanded of them by society at large. Sometimes this has been because the necessary resources have not

---

*S's baby boy has developed a rare muscular disease for which there is no known cure, she has left her job and spends most of her time looking after her son. She has recently set up a support group for women living in the local community who have handicapped children.

been made available. At other times teachers have been reluctant to abandon educational strategies that they have tried and tested over the years. Even now schools are hesitant to discuss unemployment with their pupils, fearing that they will become demotivated for the remainder of their time in school. The consequence of this lack of response is that pupils continue to pursue irrelevant educational courses and leave school ill-equipped to handle the reality that awaits them. For a girl, this reality is likely not only to include a broken marriage and a period of single parenthood but also an average of thirty-five years on the labour market after the birth of her children. Paid employment is going to be vital to her well-being as an adult. Schools today can no longer ignore their responsibility for ensuring that girls are well prepared for personal and economic independence.

In recent years, the vital links between women's educational opportunities and employment prospects have begun to be recognised. Legislation in the form of the Equal Pay Act and the Sex Discrimination Act has provided women with the right to ask questions and take action — sadly, they often do not have access to ways of ensuring that their answers are listened to and action taken is appropriate. In 1976 the Equal Opportunities Commission (EOC) circulated all Local Education Authorities (LEAs) with details of the effects of the Sex Discrimination Act (1975) on local educational provision for girls and boys. Many LEAs have since gone some way towards reviewing their secondary school timetables to ensure that craft facilities are equally available to both sexes — but they have not been obliged to move beyond this, to an examination of the 'hidden curriculum' and a questioning of the traditional sexist ethos of their schools. Individual sex discrimination cases have been equally limited in their effect, although they too have helped to provide a context for discussion which teachers had previously entered at considerable personal and professional risk.

Almost a decade since the legislation came into effect there is now concern at ministerial level about evidence of sex inequality in our schools. In November 1983, Sir Keith Joseph, Secretary of State for Education, stated:

> 'The facts are disquieting. At all stages of the educational process girls fail to reach their potential in these subjects.... They are handicapped both in their opportunities for employment and indeed in aspects of everyday life which require a grasp of mathematical or scientific concepts.
>
> Facts such as these show that many girls are not reaching their full potential in important areas of study. They are therefore cut off from some of the most promising opportunities available to young people

seeking employment. To that extent, the education they receive is inadequate. They are entitled to expect better.'
(*Times Educational Supplement* 18/11/83)

In 1980 the Schools Council, in response to an EEC directive, had drawn up an 'equal opportunities' policy statement and subsequently committed funds to a national project to 'Reduce Sex Differentiation in Schools' (1981-83). The report of this project (Millman and Weiner 1984) describes the escalation of interest in sex equality amongst educationists during this period and the level of sophistication that has been reached by many teachers working at classroom level to develop strategies to promote the educational success of girls. A national network of teachers has now been established to exchange information and examples of good practice, and some LEAs recognise that a commitment to equal opportunities demands more than a commitment to timetabling changes! Today it is true to say that 'equal opportunities' is placed tentatively on the national educational agenda although the priority it takes and the resources allocated vary enormously from one LEA to another. Such disparities depend on a number of local factors, from economics and labour traditions to the whims of educational administrators and the expediencies of politicians. These factors must determine local strategy and at the same time underline the need for close co-operation between all organisations concerned with the quality of girls' education. Teachers who are now devising ways of capitalising on the currently high level of national awareness need all the help they can get to obtain a commitment to positive action with their local authority.

Obtaining A Local Commitment To Positive Action: Raising Awareness — A School-Based Approach

It is only in the wake of publicity about research reports and positive action projects that many teachers have begun to identify the problem of sex inequality in their schools. Previously they have believed themselves to be deeply committed to the concept of equality of opportunity and they are shocked when they come to realise the discriminatory nature of many traditional classroom practices.

Raising individual and institutional awareness of sex differentiation must therefore be a first stage of any long term strategy to achieve equal opportunities in schools. Many adults reach this awareness through experience of antagonism in their personal relationships, later making links with institutionalised sex differentiation. For others, the relationship has to be demonstrated through discussion of examples and examination of statistical evidence.

In some schools, individual teachers have succeeded in demonstrating these links to colleagues. They have collected examples of sex differentiation from their own classroom practice and compared their observations with those of colleagues. Sometimes a small group has investigated the problem systematically, collecting examples of sexist resources or statistics about subject choice, exam passes and career destinations of pupils. In many cases, when such facts have been collated and discussed with other staff, Heads have been persuaded that there is a genuine educational problem which merits further investigation. Working parties have been subsequently set up to monitor the performance of girls and boys in certain subject areas and staff have been asked to examine resources and teaching approaches at departmental level.

It usually takes a school at least a year to progress from initial investigation to courses of positive action. The process can be speeded up, however, if schools receive interest and support from individuals and groups outside the school. Very often teachers need to obtain additional factual information, about youth training schemes or family planning programmes for example. Or they will be looking for individuals who can contribute to staff in-service training programmes on such topics as 'The needs of Asian girls' or 'Opportunities for girls in local engineering'. In very few areas are there yet established central resource banks from which teachers can obtain information catalogued on a gender basis. Nor do they have ready access to a local contact network from which they can obtain names of speakers who could contribute to in-service courses or even to the school's social studies or careers programmes. Women working in non-traditional jobs or those who have reached positions in senior management are welcomed by many schools as positive role models for girls who are making their subject choices in their third year.

For schools who have thoroughly investigated the problem and identified certain courses of action, there is a greater need than ever to look outside for guidance and expertise. Such schools need resources both for pupils and staff and often they have great difficulty in finding these in their teachers' centres, libraries and local bookshops. Sometimes this is because traditional index systems are inappropriate to their needs but more often there is a real lack of suitable materials. In these circumstances libraries can be asked to put together appropriate book collections, bookshops can be asked to order non-sexist books. But most usefully teachers and parents can meet together to compile booklists and to collate teaching materials which can be reproduced and distributed through the local teachers' centre. For schools who see their responsibilities extending beyond the traditional curriculum, staff expertise is often needed in extra curricular activities — people to plan a 'girls' input into residential weekends, youth clubs, play schemes and activity days.

Raising Awareness — A Community-Based Approach

Where local schools have not taken positive steps to address the problem of sex differentiation, the initiative has often had to come from outside. Sometimes the issue has been raised by individuals contributing to professional training courses either in teachers centres or in higher education institutions. Health education, for example, provides an excellent forum for discussion of sex roles and interpersonal relationships, through which teachers can be encouraged to investigate their own resources and counselling techniques on their return to school.

For parents who are worried about the education of their daughters, it is sometimes difficult to find a way of raising the issues with teachers without causing unwanted attention and considerable embarrassment for the girls themselves. Often class teachers refuse to recognise signs of sex inequality and parents are persuaded to let the issue drop. In these cases it is useful for parents to join together with others from the same school or other schools nearby. Working through the parent teacher association (PTA) or the school's parent governor, it is possible to raise such questions 'officially' and Heads feel obliged 'to be seen' to take the issue seriously. In these situations it is worth preparing the ground carefully before getting the item onto the meeting agenda — local facts and figures, as well as carefully worked out arguments presented within the framework of 'the law of the land', are often necessary to get past the initial barrage of hostility. Many Heads find it hard not to agree to 'look into the matter', and a proposal to set up a working party composed of staff, parents, governors and members of the local community is likely to be favourably received.

In areas where democratic inroads into the school's curriculum are not easy to find, a context has to be created in the local community which exercises some influence on staff, parents and pupils. Sometimes community groups do not have to exert direct pressure, but can simply act by example. On hearing about meetings and projects which recognise the needs of women and girls in the local community, teachers are often delighted to learn that they are no longer alone in their concerns and they find the courage to raise questions in their own institutions. Broad based equal opportunities groups can provide such teachers with the initial support they need, working closely with social workers, youth workers and parents for example. Later they can form subgroups to discuss strategies for developing opportunities in each area of interest. An 'education' group might decide to produce classroom resources, set up an equal opportunities panel in its local union branch or approach the Teachers Centre to ask for support for its activities e.g. to resource a one-day conference for other interested teachers. At this stage it is useful to maintain links with people working in related fields, not only for moral support but to provide a regular exchange of information and ideas. In some parts of the country an 'equal opportunities' newsletter has served this purpose and has also focused people's attention on the escalation of activities in this area.

Imaginative use of the media, both radio and newspaper, can do much to raise awareness of the issue of educational equality. Regular publicising of local initiatives, however small, together with discussion of the reasons for taking positive action for girls, has certainly encouraged parents to look more critically at sex differentiation in schools in recent years. This has been the case even where the projects concerned are not directly related to schools. Courses for women returners, for example, have raised questions in women's minds about the inadequacy of their own secondary education, and therefore that of their daughters.

There are many opportunities for such projects to make direct links with local schools, even if this is only at the level of asking Heads to distribute leaflets through pupils, advertising language classes, evening classes and counselling sessions at the local community or women's centre.

Some Manpower Service Commission (MSC) funded projects for unemployed 16-19 year olds have approached school careers departments for names of girls who have left school and who have been unable to find work. In urban areas outreach workers have received funding to visit young women in their houses. Later they have set up local 'drop-in' centres for those who have become isolated, or support groups for those who are pregnant or who have young children. In LEAs which already have a commitment to Community Education, the establishment of school-based creches has enabled young mothers to attend day classes. Some authorities are currently investigating new ways of opening up their facilities to the public, in an attempt to offset the effect of falling rolls — proposals for school-based community projects, funded by outside bodies, have been positively welcomed by such LEAs.

In recent years, school awareness of sex inequality has been successfully raised by individuals from local organisations and institutions. Researchers from university social science departments have offered support to students wishing to conduct research projects on equal opportunities, looking at attitudes of local employers to girls entering non-traditional jobs for example. Research results have been forwarded to school careers departments and the central careers office, and these have succeeded in generating an awareness that did not previously exist. Engineering and computer science departments of higher education institutions have also launched joint initiatives with schools and sixth form colleges to encourage more girls to move into science and engineering. One-day conferences held at polytechnics have stimulated many schools to examine their own records of girls' success in these areas and search their curriculum for reasons underlying the imbalance between boys and girls.

Although the majority of schools are resistant to explicit attempts by outside bodies to influence their curriculum, individual teachers generally welcome the offer of resources which give added stimulus to their lessons. Local theatre groups have now devised a number of ways of using traditional themes to raise discussion of equal opportunities, and many are willing to put on drama workshops at local schools.

Local solicitors or Law Centre groups who have drawn up leaflets about equal opportunities legislation have found these have been welcomed as a resource in social studies and careers education programmes. Media resource groups meeting at local community centres have produced photographic packages of local women and girls which have been displayed in reception areas of schools and used as a stimulus in CSE and 'O' level English Language classes.

Moving towards Positive Action in the LEA

Examples of small scale initiatives are numerous and vary in their local impact. What is certain, in the present climate of heightened awareness of sex inequality in education, is that with effective co-ordination and imaginative organisation they provide a range of ways of introducing equal opportunities into the arena of local education policy.

This has been successfully achieved in a number of LEAs which are enormously diverse in their political and educational complexions.

Although in a couple of LEAs it has been the local politicians who have initiated a programme of equal opportunities developments in local schools, in most cases they have responded to an educational need expressed by teachers and administrators. Some LEAs have responded positively to the findings of school-based working parties. They have assisted in the dissemination of a school's findings by backing conferences to which staff representatives from local schools are invited. Sometimes this has led to the establishment of an LEA working party looking at equal opportunities across the curriculum or concentrating on particular curricular areas such as Craft Design and Technology, Computer Studies or science. In other cases specific projects have been proposed and funding bodies have been approached to join the LEA in sponsoring action research in a particular subject area. The EOC has supported a number of such projects and will continue to do so despite stringent reductions in its budget. In some of these cases the LEA has agreed to continue supporting the initiative after the jointly funded project has ended. This has required a considerable commitment from the authority at policy level, and indeed, three of the country's hundred-odd LEAs (namely ILEA, Brent and Haringey) have now not only declared a policy commitment to equal opportunities in education but have also appointed advisors to support local teachers who are responsible for implementing policy at classroom level. LEAs with this level of policy commitment are continuing to evolve positive action strategies suited to their local situation. In all cases in-service training of teachers takes a high priority and a variety of models have been adopted to try to ensure that good practice is shared and developed by teachers at all levels in schools. One LEA has asked a senior member of staff in each secondary school to take responsibility for co-ordinating the equal opportunities policy throughout the school and it is extending its in-service provision and curriculum review to local primary schools. Positive action, on any significant scale, usually starts in secondary schools where there is clear evidence of sex differentiation in subject and career choice, although parental initiatives can often be introduced in primary schools where teachers welcome practical parental assistance in the classroom. Often the raising of awareness at primary and secondary level requires a different approach, although the ultimate goal of formulating school policy, reviewing the curriculum and adopting a course of positive action remain common to both.

It is undoubtedly true that in LEAs publicly committed to sex equality in education classroom teachers are able to take up the issue more confidently and tackle it more effectively. This is not to say that teachers will always want to commit themselves directly to obtaining a policy commitment from the LEA. Many prefer to concentrate on changing practice within individual schools and look to others to take the issue forward at a broader level and through other channels. This multifaceted approach to raising awareness and formulating policy, combined with the promotion of examples of good practice in schools, has proved to be successful in a number of areas. It is perhaps in this context that teachers most need to look to individuals and organisations outside schools. It is vital that local networks are built up through which the numerous initiatives are co-ordinated and upon which those working towards sex equality in schools can depend for practical commitment and support.

References
1. Assessment of Performance Unit (APU) *Mathematical Development, Primary Survey Report No.1* 1980
2. Chasen, B. Sex Role Stereotyping and Prekindergarten Teachers in *What do you expect? An Inquiry into self-fulfilling prophecies.* Insel PM and Jacobs in LF Cummings: Calif 1975
3. Connor, Shackman and Serbin *Child Development,* 1978, 49
4. Douglas J and Cherry N *Does sex make any difference?* Times Educational Supplement (9.12.76)
5. Girls and Technology Project (GATE) *Sexism found in CDT Timetable* Times Educational Supplement (7.10.83)
6. Hargreaves, D *Sex Roles in Divergent Thinking* Brit. Journ. Educ. Psycho.. 47, 25-32. 1977
7. Harvey J. *Children's Expectations and Realisations of Science* Brit. Journ. Educ. Psychol. 50-1980
8. Hodgeon, J. *Sex Differentiation in the Nursery School* (unpublished paper) Cleveland LEA 1983
9. Kent, L. 'Are examinations up to the mark?' *NUT Secondary Education Journal,* NUT 1982
10. Kohlberg A Cognitive-Developmental Analysis of Children's Sex Role Concepts and Attitudes in E.E. Maccoby (ed). *The Development of Sex Differences* 1966.
11. Millman, V. *Double Vision — The Post School Experiences of 16-19 year old girls* Coventry LEA 1982
12. Millman, V. *Teaching Technology to Girls: a Workshop Approach* Coventry LEA 1984
13. Millman, V. and Weiner, G. *Reducing Sex Differentiation in Schools — A Schools Council Project* Longmans 1984
14. Millman, V. & Weiner, G. *Sex Differentiation in Schooling: Is there really a problem?* Longman 1985
15. Mischel, W. A Social Learning View of Sex Differences in Behaviour in the *Development of the Sexes* Maccoby (ed. 1967)
16. Orr, P. Sex Differentiation in the Curriculum *NUT Secondary Educational Journal* NUT 1982
17. Schools Council *Options for the fourth* Schools Council 1982
18. Serbin, L. Teachers, Peers and Play Preferences: An Environmental Approach to Sex Typing in the Pre-School in *Perspectives in Non-Sexist Early Childhood Education* ed. Spring, Teacher College Press 1978
19. Spender, D. *Invisible Women* Writers and Readers Co-operative 1982
20. Stanworth, M. *Gender and Schooling* Hutchinsons 1983
21. Wood, R. Sex Differences in Answers to English Language Comprehension Items in *Educational Studies* Vol 4 No.2 June 1978
22. Whyte, J. *Beyond the Wendy House* Longmans 1983

CHAPTER FOUR

Young Women And Work: Careers Officers' Perspectives
Olivia Grant and Linda Moore

Young women, and indeed any women, when faced with the need to seek vocational guidance will inevitably find that their sources of help in this sphere are severely limited. Since the demise of the Manpower Services Commission's Occupational Guidance Units, the Local Education Authority Careers Service is now in the position of being the sole agency with staff professionally trained and appointed to offer a range of services associated with the provision of vocational guidance. The bulk of the Career Service's work is with young people between the ages of 13 and 19 years and in some Services special provision is made for Polytechnic, Technical College and College of Education students as well as discontinuing students. Equally, in some Services there is the provision for adults to seek vocational help and guidance but this is determined by the resources available locally and does not constitute any standard provision.

The Careers Service's *raison d'etre* is to offer vocational advice to young people on an individual or group basis, though the bulk of its work is orientated towards the one-to-one individual interview. This help is available to young people whilst at school and in their early years of work, training or, indeed, unemployment during which time the Service seeks to act as an intermediary between its clients and the world of work and training or further and higher education. A vital aspect of its role in this process is the gathering and provision of a wide range of information about jobs, careers and training and many services have set up libraries and resource areas which are open and available to the public, either as part of the guidance process with a Careers Officer or to be used independently by the individual who is in search of information only.

For the Careers Officer, the context in which vocational guidance is given must necessarily reflect knowledge, awareness and understanding of the employment and training opportunities available. This is equally true whether a client is intending to leave school at 16 or hopes to continue and pursue a course of further or higher education which will mean delayed entry into employment. Each Careers Service is locally organised but is part of a national network and therefore has detailed knowledge of the local situation, ready access to regional information and potential access to national information also. The Careers Service's knowledge of the local situation is used by its Officers to give meaningful and relevant individual advice to young people during the time that they are making decisions about their future and young women, as well as their male counterparts, are thereby made aware of the extent to which job opportunities have declined or expanded in their particular locality. It should come as no surprise to say at this point, that for many young women of 16 there are currently fewer opportunities for jobs of all kinds in most regions than were available ten years ago and, in many instances, women who wish to enter employment areas that were traditionally the domain of men are consequently more restricted not only because of prejudice and discrimination but also because of the real lack of job opportunities. This is therefore often the context in which vocational advice is being offered to young women and attempts by Careers Officers to give realistic guidance based on this situation have sometimes been interpreted, rightly or wrongly, as discouragement or discrimination.

Even given the situation of diminishing employment, however, Careers Officers take very seriously their obligation to make young people, irrespective of gender, aware of the whole range of opportunities available to them, though they are often discouraged by the reaction of clients and their parents when introducing less traditional ideas into the guidance process. It is not at all difficult to bring to mind the looks of disbelief on the part of female clients at the very suggestion of pursuing training or a job in non-traditional areas and be forced to acknowledge that the more traditional views of parents and friends can so easily dissuade the young girl who might otherwise have been tempted to be more adventurous in planning her career.

However generously it is staffed, the Careers Service must concede that it will still have only a comparatively limited contact with young women and by far the greatest influence on their vocational thinking and choice will be their parents and relatives, friends and school. It cannot therefore be too strongly recommended that girls and their parents are offered the fullest access to the widest range of careers information and advice before choosing their CSE and 'O' level subjects at the crucial age of 13 years, if not before this point. Without appropriate and informed choices being made by girls at this stage it will be virtually impossible for a Careers Officer, however committed, to assist a girl to get a job for which she has not obtained the necessary skills and qualifications.

This, of course, highlights the dilemma faced by girls, teachers and Careers Officers when confronted by the situation where places on courses for certain subjects are not available or limited by teaching time or classroom facilities. These practical limitations are often determinants of subject choices and are therefore the future limiting factors in a girl's ultimate job or career choice.

One of the other crucial points of contact with the Careers Service for girls will be during the fifth form, though in many areas girls will have attended talks and interviews given by Careers Officers during their fourth year and, by this stage, much careers information should have been assimilated. Careers Teachers too, will have had a substantial role to play during this period.

It is very difficult to assess or understand the reasons why young people change their vocational thinking but it is noticeable to Careers Officers that girls, in particular, become more limited in their expression of job choice by the time they approach fifth form school leaving stage. In careers interviews, at this point, many girls reject their sometimes more progressive careers thinking of the third year. It is not unusual for girls to express great surprise when reminded of the jobs which had interested them only two years before. A Careers Officer attempting to re-kindle this type of interest is often met with good humoured cynicism and statements which imply that the girl is far more realistic, has now "grown-up" and chosen something far more sensible (often more conformist!). Careers Officers are often fearful of alienating such young women by pressing something now felt to be inappropriate by their interviewee and therefore understandably feel obliged to draw back and continue with an interview which more suitably reflects her perceived needs. An outsider may feel that a Careers Officer who opts for this course of action is failing to grasp the nettle. However, a Careers Officer's prime responsibility is to respond to the needs of an individual client and the protection of the relationship which such action should create will hopefully allow room for later and subsequent contact in which the young person has the opportunity to change and grow. After all, this growth may well be towards active consideration of non-traditional occupations.

Outside of the young person's own wishes there are often other imposed constraints not the least of which is parental choice. How often has a Careers Officer been confronted with benign fathers smilingly disclaiming the importance of continuing education to their sons and its irrelevance to their daughters or equally declaring the unsuitability of certain male tasks for their daughters who should really not be subjected to the bad language of the engineering workshop or who couldn't cope with the heavy lifting involved in something like the building trade. Expressions of this sort are often confirmed by mothers and accepted by daughters.

These prejudices are often reinforced by the experiences which young women have in attending interviews for jobs and training schemes. Despite the introduction of legislation pertaining to Sexual Discrimination, an analysis of placings made through Careers Officers is unlikely to demonstrate much change in recruitment patterns. It is still predominantly young women who move into secretarial and sales work and young men who become engineers and construction workers.

The situation is further exacerbated in areas of high unemployment by the role that an unemployed girl is forced, or seeks, to play within the family. The care of children and other relatives (sometimes the elderly) together with shopping and housework offer much to occupy a young woman and may be seen as more real and tangible expressions of purpose or role than can be gained by visits to Careers Centres and Job Centres. For these young women it often seems that there is little to be achieved by seeking vacancies which do not exist for them and spending money in what would appear to be a futile search. When questioned about their motivation in undertaking such domestic responsibilities many girls state this enables them to make a contribution to the family, gives them status within it and sometimes affords mothers and sisters the opportunity to take up part-time or shift work which is denied the recent school leaver because of her age.

Not all girls make this choice and even those who do may only take on the domestic role for relatively short periods of time. When young women do actively seek work many find it within the traditional areas of employment and are perfectly happy with this. However, for the young woman who wishes to become a motor mechanic, an engineering or building trades apprentice, for example, there are a number of obstacles to be overcome before such aims can be achieved. It is crucial that a young woman seeking such work has been enabled to achieve the correct qualifications and has had the opportunity to acquire the necessary skills training before presenting herself to an employer. It is also vital that girls are aware of the age restrictions placed upon potential trainees and apprentices in such areas as building and engineering. This militates against a girl who discovers some while after leaving school that she would have the interest, confidence and ability to take up an area of non-traditional work as has been mentioned. The needs of women in this context should be recognised by employers, trade unionists and training boards when deliberating the future of apprenticeships and adult training and re-training needs.

As has been indicated at the beginning of this chapter, the Careers Service is fundamentally an intermediary between the world of work and its clients. A realistic assessment of its role would not allow the Service to believe that it can change radically the socialisation process which its clients, both young people and employers, have undergone. What it can aim to do, however, is to promote the idea of equal educational opportunity to male and female alike, to encourage young people to use such a base as a stepping off point into the widest range of education, training and employment opportunities. There is evidence that employers can be convinced of the value of recruiting young women having once experienced the employment of suitable female candidates. These factors are interdependent. Suitable candidates must be suitably qualified and have horizons wide enough to encompass non-traditional ideas. The role of the Careers Service is to facilitate, encourage and promote this.

CHAPTER FIVE

Why Work With Girls?
Judy Seymour

What is Wrong with the Youth Service?
Although it has been widely assumed that the coming of state education, and more recently, of comprehensive education, has guaranteed equality of education for all, equality of opportunity has come in only a small measure to the girl workers denied day release, to the girl who is offered less mobility within curricular structure than her brother, to the women who are denied further education, and to the women who are denied re-training, because they are married, and therefore 'kept' by their husbands.

This disparity in education is also to be found in the Youth Service.

The Thompson Report on the Youth Service in England, 1982, states: 'faced with a wide spectrum of needs, we must state as a first principle that the Youth Service has the opportunity and the duty to help all young people who have need of it.... the Youth Service, as we have found, believes strongly in its educational role, with emphasis on the principle of 'learning by doing'. We see the Youth Service as deeply educational, in that it should be helping young people to become whatever it is in them to be'.

But who are the people who decide for young people 'what it is in them to be'? Within the Youth Service, around 82% of the full time workers are male. Since it is the full time workers who have access to training, and who make decisions about programming, timetabling, and the allocation of resources, it is men who can develop their skills, and men who make the important decisions.

We know that there is a strong relationship between teachers' expectations and the actual behaviour of the children they are teaching. We also know from studies carried out with babies that adult behaviour towards them is conditioned by whether they believe them to be male or female. It is therefore not surprising that the present distribution of resources in the youth service is unfairly distributed in favour of boys. Unfortunately, those full time workers who make all the decisions, are, on the whole, very reluctant to acknowledge that there is any bias in the work they do. Most of them adhere to the belief in a *homogeneous* grouping of 'young people' whose needs are being equally met.

Our expectations of young people play a big role in the decisions we make about the ways in which we relate to them, and more subjectively, about how we seek to influence them. Many organisations for young people seek a more democratic approach by consulting and involving the young people in decision making. This may take the form of token representation on management committees, or a more genuine devolution of power. Unfortunately for the girls and young women who do attend the local youth club with its liberal philosophy of helping young people to be what it is in them to be, the boys will outnumber the girls three to two, and in the words of Thompson, 'the boys are much more conspicuous than this proportion would suggest'.

In short, the Youth Service uncritically mirrors sexist attitudes in society. The Thompson Report is the first government review of the Youth Service since 1970. Its immediate predecessor carried little weight with the government of the day, and the Thompson Report looks set to be of equal insignificance. Completely devoid of any political analysis, it fails to note that the present political climate is hostile to much that it hopes to see happen. It does however acknowledge that sexism and racism are dominant in the attitudes of the young, and thereby gives official recognition to those workers who wish to challenge the present system. Throughout the sixties and seventies, there have been numerous studies of boys at school, friendship groupings, academic performance etc., but attention has been drawn to the fact that there is an appalling lack of literature concerning the adolescence of young women. Youth culture is treated as synonymous with male youth culture. In her book on Women and Education, Eileen Byrne said: 'we should begin to make socially unacceptable the common attitude of triviality and mockery which so far has characterised the public reaction to the intelligent questioning by a few in the leadership of education as to why the education of girls should be any different to that of boys'. This was in 1978. In 1982, Thompson acknowledges that the Youth Service should 'take deliberate steps to put right the sexist elements of its practice and philosophy'.

Since the report also cannot decide whether 'current resources are sufficient to meet the needs', thereby ignoring the research recently undertaken by Doug Smith for *'Youth Service Partners'*, which vividly demonstrates how recent cuts have damaged the service, it is no surprise that the government has been able to claim that as money does not figure in the Thompson Report and recommendations, it is assumed that it is not of primary importance to the service. Thompson states that 'one of the most important needs is to correct the present imbalance between men and women in the full time worker and officer force'. If, as the report argues, present levels of provision are to be maintained, one wonders how this is to be accomplished without an increase in staffing levels and positive discrimination in favour of women when job vacancies do occur. Once again, the ruling class may acknowledge the existence of inequality, but it will be up to those who suffer the oppression in their daily lives, to effect the change. Freedom comes to her who takes it!

In the Past

For those of us who, denied access to the history that would prove otherwise, view the 20th century as a steady progression away from Victorian values and into a new age of equality and enlightenment, the history of the Youth Service offers some interesting insights. Feminists have taken upon themselves the difficult task of rooting out some of the facts and figures which give lie to the sentiment that 'we've never had it so good!' Anyone who is interested in pursuing this to the full should start by reading an article in *Youth in Society*, no. 79, called 'Reclaiming the Past'. This research, undertaken by a group of feminist youth workers, shows that the lack of energy put into girls' work has been a feature of the Youth Service only since the 1950's, and that the disappearance of work specifically with girls can be traced through the history of its national organisation. In 1911, the National Organisation of Girls' Clubs was formed, which, in its first year had 40 county or branch unions representing hundreds of clubs, and 70 individual clubs affiliated. In 1934 it was re-named the National Council of Girls' Clubs. Its constitution mandated it to 'undertake investigation and to arrange deputations to Government departments and public bodies such as the local education authority, in connection with the social, educational and industrial needs of girls and women, and to bring the council into closer touch with such bodies.'

It next became the National Association of Girls' Clubs, and in the 1940's, the National Association of Girls' and Mixed Clubs. Girls finally disappeared from the title in the 1950's with the establishment of the National Association of Youth Clubs. Almost thirty years later, in 1979, the NAYC established the post of girls' work officer. One worker was appointed with secretarial help, to develop work with girls and young women nationally!

Several factors contributed to this series of events; most notably, the post war enthusiasm for mixed work, and the growing professionalism which led many men towards youth work as a career. Undoubtedly, pressure from young people themselves played a part in the establishment of mixed facilities, but the consequence has been that girls have been neglected, and now that girls are a minority within the youth service, and women workers are also a minority, officialdom admits to there being a 'problem'.

Issues Facing Women Youth Workers

The issues for the woman youth worker are complex. The factors against her succeeding in challenging sexism and introducing positive ideas into her work with young people along these lines are numerous and depressing.

Seven hours a day, five days a week, young people are in full time education. A youth worker in a club setting, apart from school holidays, may spend a couple of hours a night with a group of, say, 12-16 year olds. If a girls' group exists, the girls may meet one night a week for a couple of hours. A drop in the ocean then, compared to the time spent in educational institutions. But the education system, particularly secondary education, seems to have serious doubts about what it should be trying to do. Faced with the complexities of the twentieth century technical age, the realities of unemployment for a quarter of the work force, and the rapidly changing cultural values which living through such an age produces, it seems that 'it is impossible to define exactly the purpose of secondary education'. 'I was brought up that if you read Greats and had sensitivities and were fairly decent to people, you were educated. You could tell who were and who weren't. But today, teachers just don't know. It's less and less clear just what we are supposed to produce.' If this is the response from a Chief Education Officer of a large rural county controlling a budget of well over £24 million a year, (*Guardian*, Jan 7th, 1975), what should we say to the hundreds of thousands of disaffected schoolchildren for whom also there seems to be little purpose to the education system which they are forced to endure for seven hours a day? The difference being that this man was educated to have positive attitudes about his own potential, and also benefited from a far greater investment in his education than his sister might have done. This is illustrated by the fact that boys outnumber girls in the post-sixteen sixth forms, and that men outnumber women by two to one in the universities (the more costly sectors). Moreover, the disparity between the sexes widens as one goes down the social scale. 'The resources — cultural, economic, and psychological — necessary for a working class child to overcome the obstacles on the way, are very rarely expended on behalf of a girl. At the extreme end of the scale, an unskilled manual worker's daughter has a chance of only one in five or six hundred of entering a university, a chance a hundred times lower than if she had been born into a professional family'. (Westergaard and Little, 1965)

Gender appropriate behaviour and patriarchal relationships are transmitted in different ways, depending on the sexual division of labour within a given community as well as by the attitudes of parents and teachers, but all of these demonstrate the relevance of gender to the experience of girls, both inside and out of school. Whilst schools may now pay lip service to the desirability of equal education for girls and boys, the organisation of the syllabus within many secondary schools continues to group subjects within 'options' that are traditionally male or female. Thus my daughter, in her third year of secondary education, may opt for either domestic science, needlework and art, or, woodwork, metalwork and technical drawing.

Furthermore, teachers accept the legitimacy of the sexual division of labour, the monotonous future faced by most of their pupils on entering the labour market or marriage, and require that not academic success, but decent behaviour from the children, is the best they can demand.

In the present climate of recession and job scarcity, the likelihood of working class girls using their gender identity as a means of escape from the sense of futility brought about by lack of opportunity should be of great concern to us all. Teenage motherhood is one manifestation of this factor, with all its attendant features of unemployment, inadequate housing, and loss of liberty for the young women concerned.

These young women are unlikely to feel consoled by the well intentioned and often quite radical declarations which have passed through the heads of various European commissions in the last ten years.

How are we to enable young women to realise what it is in them to be, if they simply don't attend the various youth organisations which are supposedly there to help them to do this? Attendance by girls is recognised by youth workers as a problem! If membership is a problem, it also ought to be recognised that the quality of involvement by girls who do attend the club is of equal concern. The principles of the Youth Service, i.e. active participation and involvement in the organisation as a preparation for active participation in the democratic process by which the western world sets so much store, are sound principles. But what is the environment in which this learning process is carried out? Research is not available on this subject, so we can only go by our observations in the field. The difficulties become most apparent during adolescence, when the demands of attracting the opposite sex really start to exert an influence on the behaviour and social relations between young people. And it is in the youth club with its atmosphere of relative freedom from inhibiting structures that these encounters take place. It is also in the youth club that the effects of gender stereotyping emerge in stark reality. The girl who sleeps around is a 'slag' whereas the boy who 'scores' is one of the lads. The girls who fall pregnant are slags and should know better because the responsibility for birth control lies in their hands. There is no need to state that the football team is for boys only, because that's the way it's always been, but a Girls' Night is sexist, and the lads, often condoned and encouraged by the male workers, will expend extraordinary amounts of energy and cunning to disrupt it. The pool table is for the boys because girls can't play well enough, same goes for ping pong, and the women volunteers work behind the coffee bar, whilst the men keep a watchful and authoritative eye, because it is the natural order of things. Some girls and women may challenge this, but many won't, and these are the ones quoted by youth workers and policy makers alike, as a justification for traditional methods of working. 'We're all equal in this club, but girls are hard to motivate, and women don't want responsibility' etc.

Supposing these educators are right in their assumption of the innate inferiority of girls and women. What steps should be taken by all these people who educate in the formal sense in schools, and the informal sense within the Youth Service, to counteract it? In whose interest is it to maintain that half the population, and indeed, the mothers of the new generation, are only fit to fulfil a subordinate role in the organisation of society at every level?

Confronting Sexism

"Anger and frustration, consolidated and supported, is not wasted, but can motivate to action." *Eileen M Byrne*

If there were figures to show the extent of rape and sexual abuse of young girls and women, the extent of the hatred and contempt with which women are regarded, and which is condoned by male society, would be revealed in all its tragic and appalling dimensions. A group of girls with whom I have been working, organised self-defence sessions. Towards the end of the course, we had a discussion about rape. It emerged that out of seven girls, two had been violently raped, and all of them had endured sexual harassment of a fearful nature, on more than one occasion. Many women have no need of statistics to prove what they know through their daily existence, and youth workers should know by the language which is used by boys towards the girls in their club. In this atmosphere of insidious violence and intimidation towards women, how is it possible for girls to overcome a prejudice which exists at home, is legitimated by school, is consolidated by employment and training agencies, the media, and commercial provision for young people, as well as the Youth Service?

What is needed is a widening of horizons for boys as well as girls. Women have responded by using their positions as youth workers to challenge the notion that mixed provision means equal provision for girls as well as boys. Recognising the remedial work which needs to be undertaken to break the causal cycle of deprivation, they have asserted the need for girls to have special provision with female leaders. The situation which has to be remedied is nothing less than the whole social fabric. There can be little hope of making an impression on the lives of the girl for whom we are concerned unless all the institutions which have responsibility for the education of the young take positive action to formulate a co-ordinated, coherent policy.

Women have always taken responsibility for stitching together parts of society that male governments have allowed to fall apart because of their preoccupation with war and aggression. It is high time that equal responsibility be taken by men for confronting, challenging, and changing a cultural and economic system which has patently gone disastrously wrong. Men have been slow to enter the arena of sexual politics, and even slower in turning their minds towards a programme of action which could be directed at the young men whose education is their responsibility. Education for boys which permits them to develop qualities of caring and communicating, and also directs them towards a sense of social responsibility equivalent to that which is deemed natural for women, is long overdue, to the detriment of society, and possibly the continued existence of this planet.

The results of anti-sexist training workshops have shown that when asked to write down the positive and negative memories women have about their childhood, there emerges a long list which could be contained within the feeling that 'I was restricted'. When asked to think about the positive things men can remember about the lives of their sisters, very few men would have been happy to change places with them. When these same people are asked whether much has changed for the young people of today, the answer is negative. Attitudes towards women can be divided into three kinds: sexist, collusive sexist, and feminist. The majority of men and women who attend anti-sexist training workshops fall into the last two categories. But when asked the question: 'What action are you going to take to confront sexism?' at the close of an anti-sexist training workshop, the grey area between the collusive sexist and the consciously sexist attitude disappears. When confronted with all the written evidence displayed on the walls around them of the personal experiences of all those participating in the workshop, the fact that there will always be those men who see no need to take direct action themselves proves that there can in fact be no distinction made between the person on the one hand who advocates maintaining the subordinate position of women, and the person on the other who advocates the desirability of equality between the sexes, but who will make no personal commitment towards achieving it. The only difference is one of honesty.

Which Activities?

The programme of activities which has been initiated by feminist youth workers for girls demonstrates in my experience, that when given the right environment, and supportive leadership — that is, leadership by women — girls are energetic and adventurous. The activities which they chose in these surroundings do not conform to the stereotype of passive and timid. They rock climb, abseil, canoe and weight train, given the chance, and the youth worker who believes that they can and will do it. Needless to say, the numbers of girls who have access to and are able to take advantage of special programmes for girls are still few. Parental pressure may prevent them from participating, even where enlightened youth workers and LEA's do offer such programmes. Added to this, women youth workers who were not equally disadvantaged during their childhood and training are hard to find, and opportunities for women to re-train in later life are scarce.

Strategies for girls' work are emerging on a national basis. Programmes for girls' activities across the country show marked similarities, although it must be said that the disparity of access to resources available to women in the North and Scotland, compared to women working in the South, is atrocious. Amongst the areas of common interest, adventure activities have already been mentioned. These activities are immensely valuable since their very essence confounds the stereotype of expectations in relation to what girls can and can't do.

Health education is a vital area which women have recognised. Teenage girls are often ignorant about how their bodies work, and one can only surmise that the classroom situation as it exists in most schools is an inadequate forum for open discussion about topics which are of intimate importance. Our notion as to the correct relationship between pupil and teacher, the hierarchy of the teacher and the taught, sadly prevents the atmosphere of mutual trust without which such discussions cannot take place.

Self-defence is seen by many girls as a basic requirement for survival. Contrary to what might be expected, this does not consist of learning a martial art, but incorporates assertiveness training as a means by which physically defending oneself will only be a last resort. Given the terrible frequency of sexual abuse of girls and women from all classes, all schools and youth organisations should offer such teaching as a matter of statutory obligation.

The special needs of girls from different ethnic backgrounds are catered for in a small way by some local authorities, although the North East is certainly very tardy in this respect. Parallel to this, some anti-racist training for white youth workers has also been undertaken.

Heterosexism, the belief that heterosexuality is the "normal" basis for relationships, is another of the prejudices which is being challenged. This is not confined to a discussion of sexual orientation, but also seeks to re-state the importance of womens' relationships with each other, which are often undermined by the importance our culture attributes to relationships with men, especially effective during a girl's middle teens, and which results in the isolation of young mothers from any friendship network.

Encouraging girls to try traditional male crafts such as woodwork, metalwork and mechanics has also achieved some success. However, until girls are given realistic opportunities to train in these crafts at skills centres, and until employers relent their sexist practices, the youth worker is working very much in isolation, and must accept that the most she can do is to increase the girls' confidence in themselves and their own abilities.

Alongside these developments, the traditional activities also have their place, and since a girls' group, like any other organisation within the Youth Service, is a place you chose to go, activities are regulated by the girls themselves. The life of a girls' group can be anything from a few weeks to several months, and obviously much depends on the resources available in any given area. One of the most exciting features of girls' work to me is the mutually stimulating and reciprocal relationship between the girls and the women leading the groups. Introducing the concept of self-help and collective teaching/learning, to girls whose appetite for learning is so often jaded by the stale rhetoric of the classroom is a pleasure indeed.

Women who assert the need for special provision for girls are treated in the main by their male colleagues to a babble of tedious and arrogant ridicule, which whilst exposing the scale of male ignorance and fear, has also cost many a woman her job. These attempts to undermine and disperse the notion of separate work with girls as a legitimate and essential part of the Youth Service have stimulated the development of regional networks of women youth workers. On the agenda of any of these regional groups at any one time will be found a long list of items needing action. For example:

Training: identifying training which is relevant to women's needs. Initiating that training and having courses validated by the (male) officers of the Youth Service.

Campaigns: The shaping of anti-sexist policies for discussion by those officers.

Resources: The need to link with other networks in order that limited resources can be effectively shared. The need to research and provide new resources that meet the needs in hand.

Development: The need to encourage other clubs to establish girls' programmes, and to inform girls that such programmes exist, and finally, the need to re-establish the National Girls' Work Organisation in which girls and young women have an authentic voice — that organisation which our grandmothers created, and which was lost in the name of progress.

In Conclusion

It is not enough to say that girls have equal opportunities in the youth club if only they would avail themselves of the equipment. It is not enough for a senior Youth and Community official to argue that he is in favour of the best person for the job when 80% of his full time staff are male. He should ask himself, "who writes the job description which allows such a situation to exist?" It is not enough, even, to provide equal education opportunities for boys and girls if boys and girls do not chose to take advantage of it. Offering choices is not sufficient to counteract a prejudice as long lived as sexism. We must make central to our work an appraisal of how those choices are taken up based on an understanding of our responsibility to fight to extend the reality of equal opportunity.

'Working with Girls' means working against anything that confines and obstructs a person from reaching her or his potential in order to fit the needs of an exploitative society. It therefore means working on several fronts at once. It is not about having a formula, or working in a linear way towards one solution. Stereotyping people into definitions which fit an exploitative notion of what is good produces different effects depending on the cultural values of any given community. Thus class, race, gender, occupation, geography, all play their part. We must be aware of all these issues before we can begin to work out a strategy; we must find our own relationship with the oppression so that we know what we need to fight for. We must know when, and how, to facilitate someone else to fight for it. Above all, the changes we are seeking will happen through affirmative, optimistic action, not through negative reaction.

If a minority of us women have won freedoms, we have also the duty to extend those freedoms to all women everywhere, for they should not be seen by anyone as a privilege, but as an innate right.

Bibliography:

Working with Girls Newsletter, NAYC Girls Work, monthly.
Thompson Review of the Youth Service, Experience and Participation ISBN 01018660X, HMSO, 1982.
Youth in Society, National Youth Bureau. Monthly.
Schooling for Women's Work Ed. Rosemary Dean, Routledge and Kegan Paul. ISBN 07100 0576 8
Women and Education, Eileen Byrne. Tavistock 1978 ISBN 422 759708
Just Like a Girl, Sue Sharp, Harmondsworth: Pelican (1976)

PART III

Fighting Back

CHAPTER SIX

Changed Lives: The Power of Community Work and Second Chance Education

Barbara Hancock

Women and Community Groups: Some Lessons

This chapter attempts to reflect on my work as a neighbourhood community worker from 1973 to 1980 in the light of my current experience as a tutor at the Southampton Women's Education Centre.

First, I would like to try and show how new ideas springing from the re-emergence of the Women's Movement in the mid '70's affected the thinking of community workers, in particular making them aware that family life is a political as well as a personal issue.

The ideology I absorbed about my role as a community worker in the 70's was:

— that I was to work with groups for political change;
— that success was measured in terms of the number of concessions won from the local council;
— that "service orientated" groups (like pensioners groups and mother and toddler clubs) were a soft and irrelevant option that if worked with at all should be admitted to only in a hushed voice;
— that ends and political processes were all important, and it was a diversion of time and interest to talk about group processes;
— that non-directive community work philosophy[1] was to be completely dismissed as politically naive and therefore potentially dangerous.

I busied myself setting up Action Groups, and became quite proud of my collection of 'AGs' (BAG for buses, DAG for damp, and so on).

In every group, women were in the majority and in most cases were the most significant members. My experience tallies with that of Ann Gallagher[2], who found that in more "respectable" areas men held the powerful positions in community groups, and had most influence, whilst under more desperate circumstances women often took the lead. In the more respectable areas I found the trend was for fairly structured community organisations to form, with men as chairmen and holding other key positions, and with a woman as the secretary. In the areas where life was tougher the groups were usually less structured and the women were more influential. However even in these cases, in two groups comprising extremely able women the search went out for a man to be their chairman. Once found the men were only there to occupy the relevant chair, and were more or less irrelevant to the operation of the group.

The significance of women in these latter groups can be explained by the fact that:

— the issues were closer to the hearts of women — who suffered more from the effects of damp houses, or the threat of upheaval through redevelopment;

— women had the time to do the extra work necessary for the group, as well as attending meetings (the men involved in groups were often not working whether through retirement, disability or unemployment, or did shift work which meant they were sometimes available in the daytime).

— the women in these poorer areas seemed to me to be strikingly the most able members of the community. Maybe able men had long since found the resources needed to move out. I found in a long established area female members of a family remaining whilst their brothers had all "made good" and left. The women remained, perhaps because they'd stayed to look after an elderly relative, perhaps through their marriage. And in the less established areas the women were there by virtue of their husband's lack of power in the housing market, or because they were single parents and so had little choice in their housing.

Women, then, were the key members of most of the community groups I worked with. However I rarely stopped to think about the significance of their involvement (as opposed to that of men's) in the various campaigns. Our focus was "The Problem" (whether damp and high fuel bills in new council housing, or the issues of redevelopment in older housing). The women "happened to be" the community activists — the question of their sex didn't seem particularly relevant.

Around the mid '70s, following the re-emergence of the Women's Movement, community workers started to think differently about the involvement of women in community action. The reasons for women's involvement in community action, and the impact on them of that involvement, began to be considered.

"Struggle inside the family and outside of necessity go together. It was clear from interviews with women in Lambeth that for involvement in struggle in the street or on the estate, a shift in attitude to housework, home and husband was both a precondition and a result. 'As I began to go out, things indoors seemed more trivial. Oh, things are never like they used to be here. I let things go now. It used to be well turned out, all clean.' It also had a profound effect on the confidence of the women involved, the way they thought of themselves. 'In those days I had no confidence, not for that sort of thing. When you start getting involved you find you're not a cabbage any more.' 'When it comes to it — now I know I'll fight'."[3]

Not only did community workers begin to think about women's involvement, but some of the theory of the Women's Liberation Movement began to inform that of community work. The most important new insight was that the private life of individuals, in particular the relationships in the family, is not something to be ignored as relevant only to the lives of those particular individuals. Instead family lives, and the roles within families, need to be understood in the context of social and economic forces, and so are a political matter.

I became involved in a discussion of these issues through my membership of the "Leeds Political Economy Class", which began to think what all this might mean for community work.

> "What community action has always done is to concern itself with the shell of the house and its relationship to other housing shells. Hence housing action campaigns have been concerned with: repairs; damp; clearance and improvement; estate design and the financing of housing. It has generally ignored the quality of the lives that have taken place within these shells. That is, community workers have accepted the division that exists between what is public and what is private. What goes on within the family is seen as being that family's concern and even when others know what is going on, they usually pretend they don't. The actual provision of housing is however accepted as a public event, part of the collective services provided by the state.
>
> Community action therefore accepts the way that society not only creates but also labels what are legitimate areas for public concern. Even though minimal housing provision is a necessary condition for women to look after their children and men, it is the actual looking after the present workers and the next generation of workers which ... is the main function of community life. In fact community action by largely ignoring this function and concentrating as it does on the physical shell, often does little more than reinforce women in their roles as housewives and mothers. It does this by implying that because their housing is defective, they are not fulfilling their roles adequately and that if only housing conditions could be improved everything would be alright....
>
> The logic of this argument is that community action should concentrate on that which is central to community life, i.e. the position of women and the role of the family in looking after the workforce and managing the tensions created by the wider society.... Just as the

physical part of the housing produces symptoms, such as damp, which indicates there is something wrong, so do the relationships that go on in houses. The women getting pills from the doctor, the man getting pissed in the pub rather than going home. Just as an issue such as damp, once a start has been made on the immediate problem, is used by the community worker as a means to explore with people why their houses were so badly built, in the same way a start can be made in exploring why people end up in the relationships that they do. Whose interests are served by such relationships and what can they do about them?"[4]

I therefore tried to re-evaluate the community work that I was doing in the light of this new thinking. There seemed to be two possible approaches: to think about the women I was already working with in community groups, and secondly to think about new initiatives that might be appropriate. I didn't take any specific action about the first until after I had stopped working as a community worker, when I was trying to write up some of my experience. I was then living away from the areas in which I had worked, and after seeking agreement sent a questionnaire to key members of different groups asking about their experience of being involved in community organisations. I got a reasonable response to my small survey (19 out of 32). The key question was:

"Some members of Community Groups say that their Group membership has an effect on them personally, for example affecting their confidence, their relationships at home or with friends or neighbours, what they have done about their job or home circumstances, or how they see their future. Do you think that your involvement in community groups or activities has had any particular affect on you as a person?"

Most respondents mentioned a growth in confidence, for example:

"I think one learns a lot, therefore it is educational and that in turn gives one more confidence in dealing with people who are better educated than oneself. It also helps you to put over your points of view."

"Yes in that I am now more confident in my actions, and after seeing some results which can be obtained through activities such as campaigning I am more willing to become involved."

Only one respondent mentioned anything about an impact on her family:

"In some instances I have been forced to make a choice between my family and the group, where time is concerned. This has put a strain on relationships at home."

My small scale study did not show striking support for Cynthia Cockburn's thesis that:

"Whatever the action women get involved in, it always modifies, sometimes transforms, personal relationships at home. When they feel that they are in a struggle they share with other women, and that it is not just for themselves, they are prepared to 'take on' their husbands or menfolk in a way they would not otherwise do. This changed or changing relationship and the emotional effects of it always show up in women's action. Even though in the long run they may gain from it, in the short run it costs women a lot to put husband and children second. The anxiety, doubt and willpower involved are carried by women into meetings; they add to the feelings expressed there, and account also for the spasmodic nature of women's struggle."[5]

My own experience of community action doesn't really tally with this. The survey I carried out didn't support it, apart from one quote, (though the survey had its inadequacies and I might have got quite a different impression if I had been able to conduct personal interviews). However, my impression of working very closely with a number of women over several years didn't tally either. Perhaps they key issue is whether or not women perceive the action they're involved in as being a 'woman's struggle'. Cynthia Cockburn talks of women in "a struggle they share with other women", even though her examples are, like mine, drawn from women involved in housing campaigns.

Involvement in community action does change women and men, by giving them greater confidence, greater belief in their own ability, by widening their circle of friends and acquaintances, by changing the actual circumstances of their housing etc., and by providing a practical political education.

Community action therefore changed women's lives, often to a dramatic degree, but my experience was that often their families went along with, or at least tolerated, their involvement. Campaigns were often, as has already been said, about issues that particularly affected women. Therefore to take action around this was not dissonant with a woman's role as carer for the well-being of her home and family. A woman's stand for a better bus service into town, or a more humane method of rehousing in a clearance programme, did not challenge her role in the home. She might be out more often, provide more instant meals, and spend evenings writing letters to the Council, but none of this challenged the basic relations within the home of who does what, who's to be regarded as the key breadwinner, and so on. Of course there were exceptions, for example where a man couldn't tolerate his wife going out to meetings and so there was a direct challenge to family relationships. But this didn't seem to be an overriding feature of the impact on women of community action.

As community workers we had assumptions about what were

relevant concerns: public issues like housing were; 'private' issues like what goes on in the home were not. Members of community groups came to groups in which we largely influenced the agenda. In these groups, though women were in the majority, there were not only women there. Even if women were having difficulties working out relationships at home in the context of their new political action and awareness, none of us, the women themselves or other group members, would have seen these difficulties as a 'relevant' issue to raise, or the group as an appropriate context for this discussion. Joking complaints about why someone couldn't come along to the pub at the end of the meeting were about as far as we got.

A second approach would have been to set up new initiatives which from the start had as their focus the issue of women's family lives as a 'political' concern. Whilst I was a community worker I never managed to do this. At first I though I'd have a new look at mother and toddler groups — maybe, I thought, there was more to them than the old dismissive community action attitude had led me to believe. However, though I worked with a number of informal women's groups, I never managed to raise a successful discussion. I failed on two counts — first the sheer impracticality of having any rational discussion in a room where there are half a dozen toddlers. Even when we did organise a creche we never had enough commitment to it to really make it work. Secondly I still was not clear from the start about the issues I was trying to enable a group to discuss. My community work style, of gathering a group in a rather open ended way and then encouraging them to discuss what they wanted to do, was bound to fail. Without a lot of ground work and input from me the group's own assumptions (reflecting society's) of what was relevant and appropriate for discussion would have failed to raise issues about the politics of family life. These issues were almost certainly of fundamental importance to the women's whole lives, yet they were seen as private matters. Relationships at home, who does what, who controls the family budget, and so on are the stuff from which women's lives are made. Yet women feel that these issues, and others like domestic violence, are their own individual, private problem.

The difficulty seemed to me to be similar with both 'issue orientated' groups like housing campaigns, and 'service-orientated' groups like mother and toddler groups. As a community worker it was difficult in practice, and possibly morally wrong as well, to bring into a group gathered for one purpose another agenda which you had not been explicit about from the start. The question then is, what is an appropriate context for consideration of the politics of private lives.

There are now many examples of community workers who have managed to, appropriately, raise with and work with these issues. This work has been written up in books like *Women in the Community*[6] and *Women in Collective Action*[7]. The solution has generally been to gather women together about a specific problem — whether it be women's health, domestic violence, childcare or the problems experienced by women workers.

'Second Chance for Women'

In 1980 I moved to Southampton and started to work as a tutor on the 'Second Chance for Women' course, sponsored by the Southampton University Department of Adult Education. Whilst my move to Southampton was (typically!) through marriage rather than career opportunity, the 'Second Chance' course seemed to offer the possibility of a constructive and appropriate way in to thinking about the lives of women.

The publicity material for 'Second Chance' described it as "a course for ordinary women, housewives and part time workers who are interested in the world around them and especially the part played in it by women." It seemed to be trying to attract the kind of women I had worked with in community groups — I could think of several who would have been interested by it — but it was also honest about what it offered. The publicity leaflet said:

> "It's a course for women who want to probe beneath the surface to find out why, for example:
> — The most important and influential jobs in the country are still held by men and not women.
> — Why most working women today still find themselves in low paid jobs with few opportunities for promotion.
> — Why, despite 'Women's Lib', the responsibility for housework and bringing up children still falls more heavily on women.
> — Why single parents, divorced or separated women often get a 'rough deal' from the Welfare State."

The course runs for one day a week for a year (within school terms and school hours). It was free (although there is now a waivable fee). The course has the support of a well staffed and equipped creche, catering for children over the age of six months. It's a crucial facility, used by about one third of the women. Two parallel courses are run, catering for a total of 40 women. The course first started in October 1979, and each year it has attracted far more applicants than there are places. The women are all interviewed before they are offered a place, which enables a two-way exchange to see if the course is really appropriate for that woman — it isn't for those who really need a very much more basic literacy course, nor is it for those who have already done pretty well out of the education system.

The course comprises sessions looking at the functioning of society and women's place in that (the family, work, education, the welfare state, etc.) together with a writer's workshop and project groups which have in the past made radio programmes or researched women's local history, etc. Most women who start the course complete it and a substantial minority have gone from it into higher education (though the purpose of the course is certainly not just to provide a bridge into a polytechnic or university).

At the end of the 1980/81 courses I wrote up a course evaluation, based on the women's initial application forms together with the responses given in a course evaluation sheet. Half of the women on the course had no formal academic qualifications. Of those who had, these were mainly in the form of a few CSE or RSA passes. Only a minority had had more significant 'success' at school, and only one woman had had any full time higher education — a year at art college. More than a quarter were single parents, living on state benefit, and the majority would have described themselves as working class.

The application form for the course asked the women to write 'a short piece to explain why you'd like to come on this course.' In response to this question a number of themes recurred:

— Women had for one reason or another (in most cases linked to how they or those around them had seen their future role) not achieved their full potential at school.

— They could see their commitments to child care lessening, so that a career became a possibility. But they saw the need for qualifications in order to be able to get a worthwhile job. The course was seen as a starting point.

— They wanted to find themselves, recapture their own identity out of all the people they'd had to be through home responsibilities — and try to realise their own potential and become more self confident.

— They wanted to return to study, to have a framework in which to think and to discuss ideas. They wanted to learn about the world and about women's place in society.

— All made remarks on their application which showed that they were not satisfied for themselves with a horizon limited by domestic responsibilities and traditional low paid women's work. Some also made statements which showed they felt that women in general get a raw deal in society.

The common motivator, then, was a frustration at the limits of their present situation. They had seen the Second Chance course — education — as a way ahead. If I had met some of the women who applied for Second Chance in their homes, perhaps in a tower block, when I was working as a community worker, and listened to them talking despairingly of their life, I would never have thought of responding to their 'need' with the suggestion that they join a stretching class involving lectures, discussions, essay writing, etc. I wouldn't have interpreted what the woman was saying as her problem and hers alone, but the likely limit of my ideas would have been that she should get a part time job, or join a social gathering for company or help start a tenants group to take action about some of the practical difficulties of her life. Sometimes adult educators came to the areas in which I worked with offers of courses — on child development, or just possibly on welfare rights. But none of these workers expected individual intellectual excellence from working class women, nor did they expect individual commitment to learning, and since they didn't expect it, they didn't get it.

So what's different about the Second Chance course? Its remarkable success at attracting applicants, and from a group renowned for its lack of participation in academic adult education, or even in any form of adult education, has to be taken seriously.

As a community worker, I find it fairly easy to 'explain away' the reason for one group of Second Chance women applying. They are those who had already become involved in political action or community action. They were involved in Gingerbread, or the Southampton Campaign against Nuclear Weapons, or a Community Advice Centre. They had already gained confidence and an identity through their participation in these groups or activities. They were already used to discussing ideas and thinking about political issues. For them Second Chance seemed a natural progression — it offered learning linked to interests they had already developed in a practical way.

There is a second group on the Second Chance course for whom it needs more imagination to account than through the prevailing assumptions about what working class women are likely to do. This group was composed of those women who had previously joined organisations like mother and toddler groups, or who had gone to leisure adult education classes like Cordon Bleu Cookery or Keep Fit. One might account for them as 'joiners', the 10% of the population who are expected to join whatever's going. If they had gone to yoga or macramé classes last year why not this year go to Second Chance? But a look at the application forms shows that this explanation is inadequate. The only sense in which Second Chance was part of a progression was that their previous experience had led the women to believe that they must change tack. Joining Second Chance was not part of an attitude 'this year Second Chance, next year Re-upholstery'. Applying was in part a rejection of the traditional classes or clubs, a feeling that these were no longer adequate for that person's needs.

The third group of Second Chance women are the most difficult to explain away. They are the women who aren't 'joiners'. They applied for Second Chance 'out of the blue'. They were working class women, perhaps single parent families living on low incomes on a council estate — hardly someone you would expect to apply for a course organised by Southampton University! In the same way that an urgent and fundamental community issue will involve people with no prior history of community involvement or political action, so Second Chance seems to strike a strong enough chord with some women to sustain them through the application, selection and first weeks of Second Chance — all of which require not inconsiderable courage and determination. Why? Perhaps it is because Second Chance provides hope — hope that a new way of life, or new life expectation, is possible.

The characteristic of Second Chance that makes it appear significant and different to those applying is not that it is a Women's Studies Course (a course about a subject) but that it is an offer of *education*. The focus of the Course is the women themselves, their potential, their future. It's offering them what they have missed out on before: education and, possibly later, qualifications — which many of the women see as being the means to a better future.[8]

Second Chance, like participation in community action, has life changing consequences. Both Second Chance and community action change the way people feel about themselves, in particular giving increased self confidence. Both give new insights into how society operates. Both give access to new groups of friends. Community action may change the standing of that individual in the community (not always in an 'upward' direction!) But Second Chance has other effects. Whilst community action is often consistent with the expectation of a woman's interests and role in the family and community, Second Chance can sometimes be seen as an active stance against these.

Our particular society needs a certain kind of family that performs certain kinds of functions, and in which different members of the family have different roles. Through history some elements of family life have remained fairly unchanging, but others have evolved in relation to the economic demands that the particular time makes of the family. In pre-industrial society the whole family unit was involved in productive work, for example on the land, or through spinning, weaving, etc. Domestic chores and the care of young children took place amidst this, so there was not the split between 'work' and 'housework' that we know today. Women and children were involved with men in the economic function of the family. Since the industrial revolution we have seen a division between 'paid' work, which is done outside the home, and the 'unpaid' work of caring for children and any other dependent members of the family. When factories first began to replace the home based work whole family units moved into the factories. But then as economic needs changed, first children and then married women were pushed out of factories, leaving men to do the economically productive work for a family wage. Women were left at home to assume a role focused on caring and home-makeup. If women did any work outside the home, this job had to fit in around the domestic responsibilities which came to be taken as their prime role in life.

The role of women as housewife and mother without an economically productive function as well is therefore relatively recent. It's not some 'God given' way of life into which women are born — although the popular image portrayed through magazines, TV etc of a woman's role often leads us to believe just this.

The reality of being at home all day with small children comes as a shock to many women. The enforced isolation, particularly if relatives live some distance away, and having as life's focus the minutiae of child and home care shows itself through the depression suffered by many women with small children. This particularly affects those with most stacked against them in terms of lack of money, no relatives for help, poor housing and the lack of a part time job which other women often need as much for company and a change of scene as for the money.

Many women in these kind of circumstances who feel fed up and depressed tend to blame themselves. Around them are images of the perfect wife and mother — in the TV advertisements, in magazines, in the imagined lives of other women. If they want for more they feel guilty. They've got 'all they ever wanted' (marriage and motherhood) — so why aren't they happy? From conversations with women on the Second Chance course guilt — at wanting something more, at not being the perfect wife and mother, at wanting something for *themselves* seems to be a common experience.

Social work, community work and some of adult education tries to respond to 'the problem of the isolated young mother'. 'Are you fed up. Can't get out? Children under your feet all day?' say the Social Services Department posters advertising mother and toddler groups. Adult Education Centres set up daytime courses with creches offering classes in keepfit and cookery. Community workers try to help women get together to make their daily life more bearable, by improving their housing conditions or campaigning for more local shops. All of these activities may bring real light into women's lives. But none address themselves to the more fundamental questions of why women find themselves in this situation anyway. Nor, in themselves, do they present any challenge to the assumptions about a woman's role in the home, with a life focused on the needs of others. In a sense all these activities are about helping to perform this role better, for example because she's happier and less fed up with the children after an afternoon at an adult education class.

Others, more radical than I, would argue that these activities, because they essentially reinforce women's home based role, are actively dangerous and collude with the needs of capitalism to keep women quietly at home. Sometimes some of these activities do strike me as wrong, perhaps something run on an individual pathology model of why the women were finding life so difficult at home. But mostly I'm a pragmatist and feel that anything that improves a woman's lot should not be denigrated, that anything that helps bring women into contact with one another and breaks down barriers is usually a good thing, and that the changes required in society to provide a proper solution are so massive that some 'first aid', even if not part of a cure, is acceptable.

However, whilst not wanting to dismiss this kind of work, I think it is important to distinguish it from Second Chance and the various other initiatives that are different in that they do challenge soceity's assumptions about women's home-focused role.

Second Chance is a challenge because by offering another chance in education it is also holding out the possibility of another way of life — a life in which home is not the only focus to a woman's life, and is not the only way in which she can find her identity. Just by deciding to apply for Second Chance, and then by having the commitment to follow through that application, women are taking a stand about their lives. It's not possible just to 'drift' into Second Chance.

The mere act of joining the course, then, means a great deal. Once on the course it almost always holds a very significant place in the member's lives. Most talk of a growth of confidence:

> "The course has taught me to air my opinions, not just agree with everyone as I used to ... I now feel more of an individual rather than just a conglomeration of other people's ideas."

> "Confidence in myself and my ideas. The urge to question instead of accepting blindly ... I see my future now as participating in life and not as a spectator which I felt before."

In other ways, though, the course had a different impact on different women. Broadly there seems to be four ways the course has an effect on how the women see themselves and their lives: it threatened; it challenged; it confirmed or it reinforced.

One or two of the women left the course, probably because they found it too threatening. A small number of others stayed right through but clearly also found this a problem. By "threatening" I mean that these women found that the central ideas about women and the nature of society in the course jarred with their perception of reality. Whilst those who stayed learnt and modified ideas through the course, this clash in ideology continued to be experienced as a problem.

Probably the majority of the course members found that Second Chance challenged previously held assumptions. The challenge could be a threat, and be difficult, but the power of the challenge was that it rang true to the women (that was why it was disturbing). A number of women went through turmoil while they adjusted how they saw themselves in the light of their new understanding, and whilst they would have wished for more support during this process they in no sense regretted their awakening to new ideas.

For some women the course was a relief — it allowed them to be proud of the beliefs they already held by showing them how their ideas were valid and important and not crazy as they'd thought before from the messages of those around.

Some women were already confident with the dominant ideas and themes of Second Chance and so did not go through a process of change in the way they saw themselves and the world — the course rather acted to reinforce, broaden and strengthen pre-existing ideas.[9]

Conscientization

The effect the course had on many of the women seemed to be reminiscent of the process of conscientization described by Paulo Freire[10]. Conscientization is about learning to perceive social, political and economic contradictions, and to take action against the oppressive elements of reality. The object of conscientization is to enable the oppressed to more fully become human, but not by just swapping places with their oppressors. It involves reflection — an intellectual exercise — and action. The two inextricably go together: for true conscientization each of these two components leads to the other.

In an intellectual sense, I think that the challenge Second Chance posed to the women's previously held assumptions about the way the world is can adequately be described as 'learning to perceive social, political and economic contradictions'. But what about the action? 'Action' conjures up pictures of militant women marching in the street. The women on Second Chance were not (at least not jointly) campaigning or otherwise involving themselves in the stuff of community action. However, in a less obvious, though for the women concerned perhaps personally more fundamental way, they were taking action. The immediate oppressive reality is the expectation by others, and by society, of their role and future. Simply coming on Second Chance was action against this. Going on with education after the course was also 'action'. Not in the sense of 'doing', but of the meaning that the act had. For everyone, to a greater or lesser extent, and in a more or less painful way the action of going through Second Chance meant taking a stand about their lives.

Paulo Freire's ideas have, of course, been taken on board by community workers. It is easy to interpret as 'conscientization' that process which members of community groups (and often community workers themselves) have gone through when they come together about some local problem or injustice. Through taking action about it, and seeking to understand what is going on, individuals may come to see society in a very different way, and may then go on to new involvement arising from their new perception of the nature of society. A tangible example would be the tenants on a system built deck access estate whose homes were damp and impossible to heat. They came together about that problem and started to take action to improve their living conditions. A series of campaigns took place over a number of years, developing from an initial effort to get repairs done, through an understanding of the inadequacy of the whole construction process and political context in which the estate had been built, to a demand for the demolition of the estate. The awareness of the problem started with individuals, who were often blamed for the conditions in their homes ("open the windows and turn up your heating and the damp will soon go away", said the housing officials). They joined with their neighbours to show that the problem was not the fault of the individual, and later with tenants from similar housing estates in other cities to show that again the problem was the result of political decisions, and couldn't be dismissed as a local unfortunate occurrence. Involvement in these campaigns changed the individuals concerned, developing their awareness from the certainty that whatever the council said, their damp wall wasn't their fault, to a comprehension of the politics of local housing, and an understanding of the tactics of community action. Just coming together and beginning to take action was defence against 'victim blaming' and enabled those concerned to feel more in control of their own lives — more human.

Paulo Freire's understanding of conscientization can therefore be applied to both community action and second chance education. However, there are some important differences in the nature of that conscientization. I have already talked about how community action has tended not to see the 'personal as political'. The conscientization involved in community action is more usually a changing awareness of how the local or national states operate, or a new critical understanding of the freedom of the local press. But our Second Chance education has had as its focus the notion of the personal as political and therefore conscientization has been in the areas of family life in addition to a changed understanding of society. The process and impact of conscientization can therefore be very different for someone involved in community action and someone who decides to come to Second Chance. In both cases the individual is active, whether that action is demonstrating outside the local housing office, or walking out the front door and saying 'this day is for me'. In both cases the individuals come to understand themselves and their society better, and through doing something for themselves gain in their own self confidence. In community action individuals say 'why should I put up with this' — a damp house, impossibly high fuel bills, an inhumane rehousing process — and begin to understand how it is that they are faced with the situation they are — its political context. They take action, and may meet with success or failure. They may be bought off, or achieve partial gains. They have to understand how they've won (or failed to win) what they have, come to terms with their success or failure, and proceed in the light of it. All this is usually done in the context of a group, and all the members of the group are usually similarly affected by the actions of the group.

Through community action people gain new understandings, change their aspirations, and have to adapt to living with their new perceptions of reality. If you no longer believe it is your inevitable lot to live in a bleak flat, with one room unusable through damp and a heating system that leaves you penniless if you switch it on, then what do you aspire to? Don't you have as much right as the Chairman of the Housing Committee to a 5 bedroomed house out in the leafy suburb? What is 'reasonable' housing? It is a human response to focus the unreasonableness of your life on known figures, perhaps local councillors or housing officials. The groups may know that their lot is the result of a whole series of inequalities in society, but certain key figures come to symbolise those divisions. However, in these situations the conflict between people is relatively safe because it is an institutional conflict — councillors expect to be harangued, housing officials, whilst not enjoying it, acknowledge that tenants may hold them personally responsible for their lousy housing conditions.

It is here that the conscientization of second chance education is different. Here, though the way to understanding is through an appreciation that the 'personal is political', the arena for action is often in personal lives. Though the group may be going through similar processes, for each the impact is different because each woman lives out her life in a different context, in a different set of relations. Whilst the need to 'do something just for me' is common, the impact of that decision is different.

"I think the course has been a very good thing for the relationship between my husband and me because previously he was the knowledgeable one. It's good to come home and for me to tell him things or point things out to him which he never considered before. As he's got a very open mind and we think along the same lines anyway it's never led to any arguments or friction."

"I don't believe the course has changed my family relationships although it has drastically affected how I see myself and what I believe."

"The course has changed my relationships with family and friends, caused a lot of dissension and argument."

"Coming home from the course is increasingly difficult — it's almost like schizophrenia — while I'm with Second Chance women I feel 'alive' and coming home requires a complete change of personality which is more and more difficult to cope with."

The conscientization of second chance education raises the same need as does community action to re-evaluate your life, to arrive at new aspirations and to cope with meeting or failing to meet these. If you now realise that women's role in the family is conditioned by the needs of the economy, if you've looked at how women are discriminated against at work, and seen how girls are socialised through their upbringing and schooling into our pattern of marriage and motherhood, then you are going to look critically at your own experience of family life. Patterns of who does what in the home come to be seen not as some inevitable norm but as part of a whole system of inequalities in a world in which women do two-thirds of the world's work for a tenth of its income. The human response to all this unreasonableness is again to focus the blame on known individuals — the family context in which we live, and the particular people in that.

"I went through a very distressing stage when I felt like leaving my husband and kids and just clearing off on my own. It was when we did the women in the family section. I remember suddenly seeing all the injustices women suffer in life and deciding I'd had enough ... It took me a few weeks to realise that the whole structure of society would not change overnight and that I really wanted to stay with my husband and kids."

As in community action there's a need to work out a new understanding of what is reasonable, and to live with the contradictions of knowing things theoretically but often practically having to live in another way altogether. But this working out, because it inevitably has to happen in private, can be more traumatic than the kind of working out that goes on with community action. The group can provide support, and it's crucial that it does this, but in the end each woman either has to make changes in her personal life, or work out an acceptance of it, or elements of it. This involves balancing a notion of what is reasonable, with the consequences of particular action and an understanding of what can best be lived with.

Conclusion

To try to draw together the threads, I think first that the ideas stemming from the Women's Movement have positively influenced community work, not only by bringing the understanding that 'the personal is political', but also by making community workers more aware of the changes experienced through membership of community groups in how people feel and think about themselves. Community work grew up in the late '60s and early '70s almost as a defence against the 'individual pathology' model of social work prevalent at that time. Community workers tended to forget about individuals in their effort to show that problems like poverty and bad housing conditions were not the fault of particular people, but due to inequalities in society. Collective action ruled, and the impact of that action on the personal life of the individual was forgotten.

The Women's Movement has helped to make it 'respectable' to focus on the individual, by showing how family lives and personal relationships are influenced by forces in society outside the family. The Women's Movement has also shown the importance of rethinking how we live — of raising challenges about society's norms of roles and relationships.

For those working with women in the community, an appropriate question is — how do you work if you want to raise questions about the lives of women and the pressures on them? What are the most appropriate starting points to enable women to look in a new way at their lives? My experience of working both in community work and adult education, is that second chance education is a particularly appropriate means of raising these questions, whilst community action can fail to uncover the issues.

Others, I know, have found community action itself to be a potent tool (for example, see the experience of Cynthia Cockburn already quoted). I suspect that if I myself had been more aware of the issues whilst I was a community worker, and been more confident of the questions I was trying to raise, then I would have found community work to be a more appropriate tool. Perhaps the key difference would have been how I had *heard* what women said, and what, out of their conversations, I pulled out as issues to explore as part of a group agenda. If I return to community work in the future I think my work would have a different shape, given my experience of second chance education. The biggest lessons from this experience are firstly that it is easy to underestimate people's ability — if you expect too little, you help to tie people down within society's expectations of what 'a working class mum on a council estate' will achieve. Secondly, that it is important to find appropriate contexts in which to enable women to talk honestly about the day to day reality of their lives, and to help them to see the way in which their experience is shaped by social and economic forces in society. But that thirdly, it is necessary to recognise the power of this new learning — it may be a liberating experience, but it can also be fairly traumatic. The following quotations are all from women on the Second Chance course:

> "I've learnt that I am not an oddity because I am not a perfect wife and mother. I no longer feel constantly guilty for feeling dissatisfied at home."

> "....I was called a trouble-maker, and I actually believed I had some kind of uncontrollable illness, it never occurred to me until the Course (and as a direct result of what I have learned) that I had a right to feel proud of my actions."

> "For me it was a question of learning educationally and emotionally. The views and beliefs I was brought up with were all demolished, with nothing to put in their place. I went through a period of total confusion and apprehension, and I felt very much alone in this."

The experience of the last woman quoted demonstrates the importance of making sure that the women have adequate support, from the workers involved, or from each other. I have tried to show that conscientization, when it involves learning to perceive the family in a different way, can be much more difficult to cope with than conscientization that just involves, say, a changing awareness of the operation of the local state. The significance of the former kind of conscientization is shown through the way that it enables women to think creatively about their lives, to find themselves amidst all the other people they've had to be, and to take positive steps towards their future. But the 'shake up' that can be involved in this process places a burden of responsibility on the workers concerned to ensure that support is provided.

References
1. For example as described by Dr T.R. Batten in *The Non-directive Approach to Group and Community Work*. Oxford University Press. 1967.
2. Ann Gallagher, 'Women and Community Work', in *Women in the Community* ed Marjorie Mayo, RKP, 1977.
3. Cynthia Cockburn, *The Local State*, Pluto Press, 1977. pp 1977-178.
4. Leeds Political Economy Class, *The Need to Change the Way We Live*. Leeds Workers Educational Association Branch, 1977.
5. Cynthia Cockburn, When Women Get Involved in Community Action, in *Women in the Community*, ed Marjorie Mayo, RKP, 1977
6. ibid
7. *Women in Collective Action* ed Ann Curno et al. Association of Community Workers. 1982.
8. For a more detailed analysis of the theory behind women's second chance education see *Learning Liberation* by Jane L Thompson, Croom Helm, 1983.
9. From a personal evaluation of the 1980/81 Second Chance course.
10. Paulo Freire. *Pedagogy of the Oppressed*. Penguin Books. 1972.

CHAPTER SEVEN

Co-operative Learning with Women in Scotland

Alicia Bruce

Education has always been crucially influential in the distribution of life chances, and many writings have recognised its key role in how power and control are allocated. The most cursory review of history clearly indicates that men have astutely understood this reality and carefully retained control of human learning in the hands of a small elite.[1] In doing so they have condemned the majority of the populace to inferior lives bereft of power and government.

This is not to argue that education can be held solely responsible for the production of inequalities in society, but rather to maintain that the denial of education to the majority makes a key historical contribution to the construction and maintenance of inequalities. The historical legacy emphasises that models of education were encoded, throughout Europe, by a minority elite of white, intellectual males, and that the paradigms these men generated positioned future generations according to their class and gender. The education system we have inherited in Scotland perpetuated, over generations, existing social relations rooted in sexist, racist and class ideologies; so that when access was finally granted to the previously excluded majorities, the education they received was predicated on the construction and reproduction of these inequalities.

Feminists have pointed out that our contemporary education systems still use gender as a primary organisational principle, exposing females to a constant process in which their future roles are defined by sexist values. As Rich expresses it, we retain a system,

> "... that prepares men to take up roles of power in a man-centred society, that asks questions and teaches 'facts' generated by a male intellectual tradition, and that both subtly and openly confirms men as the leaders and shapers of human destiny both within and outside academia."[2]

And yet it is widely assumed, inside and outside educational institutions in Scotland today, that universal state education has now ceased to differentiate in class and gender terms. Although women continue to be under-represented in many areas of our educative systems (apprenticeships, post-graduates, technological training, etc.), many educators suggest that any gross differences in educational outcomes can be explained away in terms of females *choosing* to perceive their futures as unskilled, low-paid workers in the market or unpaid domestic labourers in the home. Spender writes powerfully to expose the hypocrisy of this oversimplification:

> "We cannot accept that women choose to have less education than men and to work in less skilled and lower paid jobs ... If women are in this position it is not because they have freely chosen it from a range of options presented to them in education, but because education has played a major role in persuading them that this is where they should be. ... Education can assist in providing an ideological framework which justifies this disadvantage and helps to make it seem reasonable."[3]

Contemporary socialist feminist critiques of education[4] argue that current educational provision offers people "equal opportunities to be unequal", and that the masquerade of 'neutral' education, open to all, cannot be accepted so long as it rests on the perpetuation of the sexual division of labour. Breitenbach[5] says of paid women workers in Scotland,

> "Their work ... replicates in many instances the work of domestic labour ... i.e. cooking, cleaning, caring for children, the sick. The sexual division of labour within the home is reproduced on a social scale, and the same attitude that women's work has little value ('just a housewife') is carried over from domestic production to social production".

Breitenbach's work points to the importance of this concept of "domesticity" in the education of females, encouraging women to see themselves as child-carers as well as child-bearers, and reinforcing their 'choice' of future work in the unskilled, temporary, low-paid sectors of the labour market.

From the feminist perspective, if the role of education systems is seen to be that of reflecting the sexual and class divisions which "naturally" persist in the structures of society as a function of the different talents and interests of individual human beings, then subordinate groups can only advance the *reality* of equality by developing, co-operatively, alternative models capable of eradicating such inequalities.

This has led socialist feminists to see adult education as a crucial arena for the development of a new educational politics to challenge the existing framework of authoritarian and hierarchically-determined role differences. Women's education is seen as part of this educational enterprise, developing initiatives which move beyond the limited and limiting expectations of traditional educational provision for females.

This then is the driving force behind many educational programmes in the contemporary Scottish scene. These have arisen not just in opposition to mainstream "schooling", but also to the rapid growth of reformist community education programmes, which are tied to the notion that programmes of positive discrimination, more socially relevant curricula, and wider community participation can, and should, create a "fairer" society.

A socialist feminist analysis of the many reports[6] which emanate from such community education programmes, reveals them as tacitly accepting traditional female roles. Most of these providers seem to work from the assumption that women, especially working class women, exist only as appendages of homes, husbands and children, and it is in this role that they are assessed and catered for.

It was against this background of compensatory educational projects in the seventies, that many women, active in feminist groups, began to develop their own alternative learning networks in communities. My own involvement began with just such an initiative in an area characterised by significant levels of "multiple deprivation" in August 1980.

Community-Based Adult Education

From its inception, this community-based adult education project received enquiries from large numbers of women, indeed the majority of participants were women with family commitments. Clearly, the provision of creche facilities, accessible locations, and flexible class times enabled women who through lack of essential facilities could not previously participate in learning groups to do so now. The project responded to this interest from women by initiating several groups in the area, tailored to the particular needs the women expressed. It should be emphasised here that these did not include what many might regard as "women's subjects"; cookery, sewing, typing, etc. The working-class women who contacted us were looking for opportunities beyond the limited expectations of such subjects, and sought an outlet from the chore of daily housekeeping and child-care, through more relevant educational provision. Some sought opportunities to obtain educational qualifications, others looked for alternative ways to develop their abilities beyond being "just a wife and mother", and valued the opportunity of a learning experience which catered for their potential as individuals.

The project faced the necessity of providing an educational curriculum tailored to these aspirations to move out beyond the traditional female roles. My own researches had shown that the women sought an education[7] which was relevant to the everyday realities of their lives, that discarded the hierarchical and bureaucratic structures of 'schooling', and that recognised their needs as mature, self-governing adults. Others, working in the network of similar outreach programmes, had made similar findings.

As the Project tutor/organiser I realised that a number of educational issues had to be tackled if an effective, relevant learning programme was to be constructed with women in their communities. It became essential to concentrate on two major questions,

1. Can we develop an alternative, oppositional educational theory and practice which ceases to perpetuate gender inequalities?
2. Given the existing deficiencies which saturate contemporary educational systems, can we develop a co-operative learning process which will begin to transform the continuing education available to women and other subordinate groups?

Trying to answer such questions led us on to some of the most fundamental problems faced by those involved in the theory and practice of women's education. These are problems of definition and function. They had to be tackled as such problems underlie, and their implications pervade, the work of women's education.

We began by looking at the existing Scottish scene: feminist education here seems to refer to two modes of enterprise. The first, commonly called 'Women's Studies', is an academic exploration of existing knowledge bases from a feminist perspective; attending to the invisibility and distortion of women's contributions in history, and challenging man-made perceptions of what is significant and worthwhile knowledge in contemporary society. The second, and closely related mode, is usually labelled as 'consciousness-raising'; a coming together of women, in cross-class groupings, to explore and validate their own everyday experience. This is undertaken with a view to developing critical awareness of women's situation in the real world and planning collective action for change.

Our national grouping of women interested in education (the Scottish Institute of Adult Education Women and Education Group) has published a number of case studies[8] which illustrate these models of women's education in practice throughout Scotland. Some of these programmes are concerned to widen the curricula and cultural character of adult education provision to take account of the class and culture of working class women. Others attempt to link feminist theory with the everyday sphere of all women's lives, analysing the relationships between existing education for women and its effects in the broader socio-economic context. Most have programmes which aim to develop an educational process which is rooted in the belief that,

> "All women are in a fundamental sense theorists, in that they are thinking, creative, social beings who can readily participate in the process of building for themselves educational networks which offer concrete choices in all dimensions of their lived realities inside and outside the family".

In developing a feminist educative process that would meet our needs in the real world, we looked at feminist projects elsewhere. Thompson, for example, seemed to be working from a similar stance,[9] asserting that effective adult education must adopt a position which "directly challenges traditional curricula and expectations for women". She insists that:

> "as educators we should recognise that when we work on the content of the education curriculum, when we discuss methods and processes, when we plan, when we draw up educational policies, we are engaged in political acts which imply an ideological choice."

and emphasises the need to analyse the content of women's education in order to ensure that it does not contribute to the socialisation of women into accepting different and unequal roles in society from those of men.

Thompson maintains that despite the claim by adult educators that they take account of women students' "needs", in reality their offerings express, consciously or unconsciously, a particular selection of the wider culture. This selection, she argues, reflects the particular social and political perspectives of an educational elite, and provides for the reproduction of sexual divisions in educational systems which perpetuates the relative under-achievement of women at all levels of adult provision. More importantly, she attempts to analyse and explain these inequalities in women's educational provision in relation to materialism, selection and control of knowledge, and social class, for example:

> "... university adult education does play a vital part in sustaining the dominant culture, ideology and social relationships of production in capitalist Britain and in doing so contributes to the sexual division of labour and opportunity which undermine the pursuit of genuine equality for women".

She asserts powerfully that the 'higher status knowledge' of universities gives them great omnipotence in the educational hierarchy and that what counts as 'worthwhile knowledge' with them directly affects the wider world of adult education and the provision available to working-class women at all levels of the educational system. Young[10] elsewhere outlines this academic notion of 'worthwhile' knowledge:

"... an emphasis on written as opposed to oral presentation, individualism or avoidance of group work or co-operativeness, ... abstractness and the unrelatedness of academic curricula, which they are 'at odds' with in daily life and common experience".

Our practice in Scotland, particularly with working class women, had clearly indicated that most women perceived current mainstream provision as irrelevant to their lives, and were alternately acquiescent to, and alienated from, most educational institutions. Certainly, adult education as presently constructed, had failed to register any positive impact on their consciousness, and their opinions, where they expressed them, described education as a middle-class phenomenon, with no understanding of working class women or their children.

We began to understand that women's education is not only concerned with such reformist notions as "broadening access to higher status knowledge" but must also develop *theory and practice* in opposition to the dominant capitalist patriarchy. Therefore, as in Thompson's programmes;

"We began with the assumption that the traditional roles of women are discriminatory and restricting ones, so that rather than offering curriculum content designed to re-affirm or reinforce them, we adopted a different definition of social relevance as our starting point."

Our aim was now clearer, to tackle the overblown status of 'pure' academic knowledge, at the same time developing alternative learning groups in real life contexts. We recognised: the need for the development of feminist theory as a *counter* force to dominant academic ideology; the importance of *what* people learn if adult education is to be a radical force in changing the unequal society; the need to construct new knowledge in active, co-operative ways and relate academic analysis closely with educational practice.

This task of analysing dominant knowledge bases, constructing alternative perspectives, and implementing these in the practical reality of women's lives, is clearly a mammoth undertaking. Indeed, opponents of such process argue that the possibility of such a movement transforming economic, political and social realities is politically unimaginable because capitalist and patriarchal ideologies are not amenable to change by such marginal, oppositional forces.

I would maintain, however, that the possibility of viable alternative forms of social life and culture is real. Women's education is not static, but continually active, incorporating and adjusting; this allows the opportunity of change through variation. The theory and practice of education and action for change can, therefore, undermine oppressive structures, through the development of active and critical politics.

The growth of educational networks with alternative values is being increasingly recognised as an important way forward for subordinate groups. Socialist feminists particularly, see this as a process of undermining traditional social authority relationships. The withdrawal of consent, by women, to dominant prescriptions for female societal roles can be identified, throughout Europe, in co-operative groupings which begin to move from "popular culture" towards more coherent insights of a "woman's place" in the world.

More and more women in Scotland are realising that they can take control of their own lives by forming such groups, developing awareness of how ideological hegemony operates, and taking action to change it, through a feminist educative process. Nancy Hartsock, from a North American context, describes this process quite succinctly.[11]

Firstly, we work on issues of everyday concern in co-operative groups, gaining collective strength by working collaboratively with other groups who share our methods.

Secondly, we work to educate ourselves and others politically in order to enable ourselves to see the connections between social institutions.

Thirdly, we develop strategies to improve our conditions of existence collectively, becoming aware of problems beyond individual ones.

Fourthly, we take action to transform existing social relations.

Fifthly, we analyse the effect of our theory, strategy and action and reflect upon their power to effect change.

As Hartsock says:

"Our political theorising can only grow out of appropriating the practical political work we have done. While the answers to our questions come only slowly and with difficulty, we must remember that we are involved in a continuous process of learning what kind of world we want to create as we work for change."[11]

This process is well understood and applied in practice by feminist adult education workers in Scotland. Two examples may illustrate developments.

A. Slimming Groups

The capitalist system makes large profits from the "slimming industry", an industry which feeds off particular images of "femininity" which encourages women to aspire to an idealised media-inspired shape. Practical feminists begin from this modern obsession with slimness and question its roots. By forming "Slimming Clubs" in local areas, a starting point for an analysis of female images in modern western societies is available. From the standpoint of everyday "commonsense" women discuss such questions as

— why do obese men not flock to slimming clubs with women?
— has anyone actually met a 'perfect' women?
— who benefits from the widespread purchase of diet foods, slimming magazines, etc.?
— is the persistent advocacy of female slimness by the media based on a concern for health or other factors?
— does constant dissatisfaction with one's body shape develop self-esteem?
— does an emphasis on the physical attributes of women enhance close relationships in practice between females?

By developing their insight into the many factors behind this wish for slimness, the media images are undermined, and women often withdraw their acquiescence to being defined and controlled by patriarchal attitudes and a capitalist profit motive.

One must of course be aware of the traps of idealism;

> "One must be sensitive to the fact that a change in women's minds does not necessarily effect change in the reality of their daily lives. Women must attempt to open routes, through education, to act to effect changes in their life choices".[12]

Most feminist educative groups are concerned to change women's lives in a real and immediate way. An individual's educational career, through co-operative learning, may illuminate this aspect.

B. An Individual History

Ann, who was employed as a domestic auxiliary in a local hospital, joined the group meetings through contact with an existing participant. Over a period of several months she gained confidence, developed social contacts, shared her skills and experience, and gradually analysed her work situation as problematic in a number of ways, which she determined to tackle.

She joined the Refresher English group relating her work to

minutes, agendas, letter-writing and grammar. This was allied to role-play of trade union meetings. The subsequent growth of skills in this area encouraged her to stand as shop steward at work. Following her election, she developed her learning through a study of women in the trade union movement, socialism, simple economic theory and welfare rights.

Finally, all the women in her study groups stood on the picket line with her during the health workers' dispute, where they argued their case forcefully for opponents and adherents alike. This led the trade union (traditionally male-dominated) to be more open to the idea of change within their branch, to facilitate the active participation of women workers.

The women who are involved in these co-operative networks recognise themselves as people who have something to contribute to communities and are increasingly active in tackling live issues: housing, transport, low pay, health, welfare rights, peace, child care, violence — the list is formidable. The important aspect of this work is not so much the subject matter as the process.

These realisations are coming to the attention of other political groupings on the Left.[13] Women, with their notions of "the personal is political" are now working with other groupings (socialists, black people, lesbians and gay men, people with disabilities, the unemployed) to develop models of a new change-orientated philosophy. The imaginative work being done in Scotland with homeworkers is an example of projects utilising a way of working which closely resembles that of feminist strategies, and the educative work that this implies.

Homeworkers in Scotland

No — not housewives who work at domestic labour in the home without pay, but "those who receive work and payment directly from a manufacturing establishment and who work in their own home".[14] The majority of homeworkers are women, usually with children, unable to engage in paid work outside the home, and frequently desperate for an income to support dependants. Most are regarded as self-employed and have virtually no protection under employment legislation, very few are unionised, and their pay is outrageously low. (The Inverallan Mill, based in Bridge of Allan paid £5 per cardigan involving not less than 30 hours' knitting, i.e. 16.6p per hour).[15] Most are isolated, and unwilling to protest against exploitative conditions for fear of losing an essential income.

Breitenbach[16] maintains:

"Homeworking illustrates to what extent women's role as carers for the young and old, the sick or the disabled, can be used to exploit them and underlines the fact that it is this domestic role that leads to their unfavourable situation as wage workers. Homework is the most extreme form of the exploitation of women as wage workers but like all exploitation of women as wage workers, it is premised upon their dual role of domestic labourers and wage labourers."

We do not know how many women are in this situation in Scotland, but it is estimated to be several thousand.[17] Certainly, there are a number of these workers in Dundee, where initiatives are beginning to tackle this problem. Here and elsewhere, community workers are contacting homeworkers, finding out about their experiences, and bringing them together for group discussions.

Utilising current research, adult education skills, trade union knowledge, participants' experience, and government funding, an analysis of the homeworkers' situation is developed collectively. Research and "writing-up" of the process proceeds simultaneously, to be disseminated to other groups in the same situation.

This work in Dundee, and other areas of Scotland, has led to the formation of a national Home Production Sales Network, which assists homeworkers with product design and development and encourages them to sell their goods outwith local areas direct to the market. Started under the aegis of Community Business Scotland, it also works to support women to set up cooperatives and train each other in the business skills they need to aim for economic independence.

Such developing initiatives[18] are part of the alliances, painfully and slowly emerging in the difficult eighties. Such projects illustrate the essential, personal "inner" elements which feminism has brought to socialism; as Rowbotham[19] emphasises, we must develop with other social groupings:

> "forms of action directed specifically towards transforming people's perception and comprehension of themselves and the world as well as being concerned with material change."

As Rowbotham and others[20] have indicated elsewhere, feminism has brought back to socialism other important contributions. In the process of developing their critique of existing educational ideologies, socialist feminists have used a form of analysis which leads to a closer unity of theory and practice. Socialist and feminist practice insists that its work must be accessible to, and relevant for, the widest possible audience.

Implicit in this methodology is a challenge to the existing forms of analysis and the clear suggestion that feminist experience has developed important insights into how personal and public resistance to dominant educational models might be developed for the future. As the collective authors of *Unpopular Education*[21] have pointed out:

"... a new politics of education will have to attend closely to the specific situation of women, and to the way patriarchal relations, in the family, in schools and in the domain of waged work, limit and profoundly shape individual opportunities for education. That is why we have insisted throughout that the forms of analysis and of politics that are needed will be both socialist and feminist."

Women have developed for themselves a feminist analysis which has the prospect of revolution as part of everyday experience. The networks which enable this are not necessarily tangible — a set of interlocking institutions — but rather a method of analysis and a way of life orientated to practical change. Ordinary women, through understanding and penetration of the economic and political structures of patriarchal capitalism, can so begin to transform them.

This is not to suggest that feminists operate only through small groups and workshops outwith the formal sector. Feminists work on a much broader front to try and transform the patriarchal order and widen the definition of what is political. As Brunt and Rowan say,[22]

"An important aspect of this transformative process has been the development of women's studies and the invasion by feminism of traditional academic disciplines. Those involved in women's studies insist that knowledge be made more accessible and more politically relevant. At the same time, women's studies aim to transform the boundaries of knowledge, by offering a critique which highlights the absences and silences of orthodox approaches. It is vital that women's studies maintain its close links with the Women's Liberation Movement. Otherwise, it risks slipping into orthodoxy and academic elitism."

They are developing a "culture" which saturates their daily lives, built from their active experience of the family, sexuality, ageing, history, media, and economics.

"Feelings and passion become understanding and thence knowledge."
Gramsci

Many Scotswomen who are participants in the co-operative networks of women's education today, would surely recognise this as a description of the process which they have developed for themselves over recent years, in the belief that all people have the potential awareness, expertise and motivation to sustain their own educational provision; and that only participants are competent to know what is important to learn in their lives. Current educational politics may characterise these developing networks as naive and marginal to the "real" educational enterprise; but recent, small-scale evaluation indicates that they are reaching the hearts and minds of a significant sector of adults, those previously alienated or excluded from continuing education.

I am convinced that the new forms of education which feminists have developed will remain significant and successful in the long term for several reasons. The first and probably the most relevant, as Firestone[23] asserts, is women's control over their own fertility and sexuality; in this area there will be no turning back. Secondly, as Hartsock says, of the feminist educative process,

> "The focus on everyday life and experience makes action a necessity, not a moral choice or an option. We are not fighting other people's battles but our own"[24]

Thirdly, and again crucially, women, as Spender[25] has made clear, now understand the significance of knowledge bases to the breaking down of the patriarchal system. This generation of feminists is ensuring that the next will not continue the fight with solely "man-made" views of the world.

Certainly, there will be many decades of transition, and few believe that progress will be steady; indeed, the present decade with its New Right ideologies advocating a return to the stability of "traditional" family values, and the erosion of women's rights in the paid labour market, marks one of the "troughs" in women's progress to real equality. Nevertheless, adult education is now developing a methodology which takes account of the real "facts of life" for the majority of the population and is concerned to enable people, as active participants not passive recipients, to become:

> "aware of, competent within, able to change, the definitive social relations of a particular society."[26]

Education, in this sense, is not "women's education", but people's education — a new, dynamic, socialist, feminist process which eradicates the sterile dichotomies of male/female; black/white; old/young; and disabled/able-bodied; and works in opposition to those powerful and active constraints of the past, towards a realisation of a quite different future.

References
1. Control of education by men is not solely an historical phenomenon. It is an incontrovertible fact that this situation pertains today, with some 97% of the government of existing structures in their control. See for example; Byrne E. *Women and Education* London: Tavistock (1978)
2. Rich A (1975) Toward a Woman-orientated University in *Women and the Power to Change* U.S.A.: McGraw Hill

3. Spender D. (1980) Education or Indoctrination in *Learning to Lose* Spender & Sarah (Eds) London: Women's Press
4. See for example: Deem R. (ed) (1980) *Schooling for Women's Work* G.B.: Routledge & Kegan Paul; Wolfe A.M. (1977) *Some Processes in Sexist Education* London: W.R.R.C. Publications
5. Breitenbach E. (1982) *Women Workers in Scotland* Glasgow: Pressgang for Glasgow Women's Centre
6. See for example: Fordham, Poulton and Randle (1979) *Learning Networks in Adult Education* G.B.: Routledge and Kegan Paul
7. Bruce A (1983) *Dominant Ideologies in Women's Education and the Search for Alternative Paradigms* Appendix 1 Unpublished M.Ed. Thesis University of Stirling
8. S.I.A.E. Women and Education Group (Collective Authorship) (1982) *Women Start Here* Volume 2: Case Studies Edinburgh: S.A.B.E.U.
   Wilson V. (Ed.) (1981) *Recent Developments in New Opportunities for Women in Scotland* Edinburgh: S.I.A.E.
9. Thompson J. et.al. (1981) *Women, Class and Adult Education* G.B.: Univ. of Southampton Dept. of Adult Education.
10. Young M.F.D. (Ed.) (1971) An approach to the study of curricula as socially organised knowledge in *Knowledge and Control* G.B.: Collier Macmillan
11. Hartsock N. (1979) "Feminist theory and the development of revolutionary strategy", in *Capitalist Patriarchy and the Case of Socialist Feminism* Eisenstein Z. (Ed.) U.S.A.: Monthly Review Press
12. op.cit. reference 8.
13. Rowbotham S. et.al (Eds.) (1979) *Beyond the Fragments* London: Merlin Press (1st Reprint 1980)
14. op.cit. reference 5.
15. idem.
16. idem.
17. idem.
18. op.cit. reference 8.
19. Rowbotham S. (1969) *Women's Liberation and the New Politics* London: May Day Manifesto Group
20. op.cit. reference 13.
21. C.C.C.S. Education Group (1981) *Unpopular Education* London: Hutchinson
22. Brunt & Rowan (Eds.) (1982) *Feminism, Culture and Politics* London: Lawrence & Wishart
23. Firestone S. (1971) *The Dialectic of Sex* G.B.: Bantam
24. op.cit. reference 11.
25. Spender D. (1980) *Man-made Language* London: Routledge & Kegan Paul (2nd Reprint 1981)
26. op.cit. reference 21.

CHAPTER EIGHT

Sweet Street Women's Courses: An Exercise in Positive Discrimination

Deborah Trayhurn

Structures of Women's Employment

Tables denoting economic activity on the part of the respondents of the 1981 British Census indicate that 40% of the total "paid" workforce in Britain are women.[1] Of these 10 millions, very few are involved in work across a range of industries. Women's activity is concentrated in eleven industrial groups. Nearly one third of all waged women are clerical workers.[2] Only 19% of all waged women work in the following areas: professional and related capacities in science; engineering and technology; managerial; security and protective services; processing metals and electrical; construction and mining; transport and storage. This statistic has not altered during the decade 1971-1981.[3] Women who do work in these areas are outnumbered by their male colleagues by over ten to one; this figure has not altered over the last decade either![4]

It is clear that the types of work undertaken by women outside of the home have not radically changed in recent years, despite the various Acts passed by governments such as the 1975 Sex Discrimination Act. Of the number of women employed as a whole, 39% are employed "part-time" compared with 2% of men.[5] The majority of these workers are employed in the following areas: cleaning; assistants in shops; clerical; domestic and school help; secretaries, typists and shorthand writers; nurses; and counter assistants. By and large women's economic activities are concentrated in jobs which are low paid, have a low status and offer little propsect of career development.

It was a widely held view that the introduction of the microchip would be a means of improving living standards and eliminating dreary working situations. The impact of technological change on women's work is of key importance, for its introduction is reducing employment in the manufacturing and service sectors where waged women are concentrated. Technology does provide a potential growth area for work, but to take advantage of this the workforce needs to be re-equipped: retraining in key areas is vital.

Looking at the figures produced by the Engineering Industry Training Board for the number of women employees in the engineering industry, it is evident that there are few who have entered this non-traditional area of employment. The figures which reflect the numbers involved and their sex, are given below.

Occupational Category	Men	Women	Total
Technician	35,840	1,804	37,644
Craftsmen	21,278	677	21,955

Source: Engineering Industry Training Board 1982.

Employment and training patterns are such that women, by and large, are confined to less skilled levels within the industry.

The task of providing training specially for women, in order to encourage more women to enter engineering, is one that is recognised by training boards such as the E.I.T.B. In 1976 the Board set up the Girls' Technician Scholarship Scheme (known as G.I.S.T.) to encourage more women to train as technicians. This interest in women and their skills is primarily focused upon the industry's need for staff which has led them to realise that by the exclusion of women a vast pool of talent remains, as yet, untapped.

Women's Training

Training in New Technology is available and for the most part is government funded, by the Manpower Services Commission. The number of women training in non-traditional fields represents only 2.5% of the total Skill Centre population, as given in a Manpower Services Review — "Practical Approaches to Women's Career Development" (conference in 1981). The Training Opportunities Programme or TOPS courses, run by the Manpower Services Commission provide a number of obstacles for women:-
1. Entry requirements place a limitation on the age of a trainee. This is often thirty years old: women who have taken a 'career break' for children may well be older than this when considering returning to work.
2. Trainees are often required to have some familiarity with the equipment and concepts being used; taking electronics as an example, many women will have been discouraged from acquiring

the relevant information and practice in Physics or Maths whilst at school.
3. TOPS courses are full-time; this in itself is a restricting factor for women if the courses do not assist in making child-care arrangements and most do not include this facility.
4. The women who have trained with government agencies have also highlighted the difficulties that they have had with an all-male course-organizing team; they mention a lack of understanding of problems related to the above factors and sometimes hostile attitudes displayed by fellow trainees and tutors alike.

One woman who was fortunate to be given a place on such a course described her experience as follows;-

> "My TOPS course was one of the good ones — there were 3 women and 17 men to start with. Then one woman left after the first two weeks and that left just two of us. We stuck together so it wasn't too bad. But the men always assumed they knew more than us, even when we got higher marks than them in exams! As far as the teachers were concerned, our main tutor was really great; as it was his first teaching job he was really enthusiastic. But other tutors were dreadful — one in particular used to invite us out for walks in the park at lunchtime and would grab at our arms when we went past. This soon became trying to kiss us — and he specifically said that he could ensure we got good marks in exams etc (which went out to employers) if we slept with him! We both decided to risk poor marks."

Some training courses can be undertaken with day-release, like City and Guilds electronics course, but as few women have entered the job market in these areas there will be few who are eligible for these courses.

In general, women who are interested in re-training, training or pre-training courses are presented with many problems which most courses on offer do little to recognise. A campaign aiming to improve the numbers of women trained by the government funded skill centres was launched in June 1984. Called the "3%" campaign, it demands measures to counter these problems.

Against figures indicating the small number of women in non-traditional training, and with the knowledge that in some areas of Europe where above-average numbers of women are employed in manufacturing women are losing their jobs at a faster rate than men, staff in the Industry and Estates Department at Leeds City Council considered the problem of encouraging more women to enter training and employment in the New Technology field. In 1982 the Council decided to set up a training course for women only. The course was to train women in the fields of electronics and computer programming.

The Sex Discrimination Act and Training

The Act allows for "positive discrimination" by employers and training bodies in favour of women where there were none, or only a comparitively small number, employed in a particular area of work. It is also lawful to provide special training for women who have been fulfilling domestic or family responsibilities to the exclusion of full-time regular employment. Leeds City Council was awarded exemption under section 47 of the S.D.A. to set up and provide courses in micro-electronics and computing for women in February 1983.

The European Social Fund

The European Economic Community, through the New Community Action Programme on the Promotion of Equal Opportunities for Women 1982-1985, has set itself the brief of achieving equal treatment and equal opportunities for women. The Council Directive of February 9th 1976 concerned the implementation of the principle of equal treatment for men and women as regards access to employment, vocational training and promotion and working conditions. The financial instrument for achieving this aim is the European Social Fund. It was decided in December 1977 to use this fund to de-segregate employment by providing financial support for special training measures designed to afford access by women to jobs where they have been traditionally under-represented. The Social Fund has a brief to provide economic support for ventures aimed to provide training for the unemployed aged between 18 and 25 (both male and female) and to provide resources to retrain women aged 25 and over.

An application was made to the Community for finance to be provided for women's technology training courses in Leeds in 1982. Leeds City Council gained an undertaking from Europe to assist in funding courses in a positive discrimination programme in Leeds. The agreement as regards the Sweet Street Skills Centre project is for each of the two parties to provide funding pound for pound. An annual application for funding is made to Europe on this basis.

The Project

Most staff began work on the courses in early December 1982. Staff allocated to the project comprise a co-ordinator, seven tutors, one administrator and a child-care co-ordinator. Staff are employed by the Industry and Estates Department of Leeds City Council for work at Sweet Street (although they are seconded to the Management Committee of the centre) and are all women. Great store is set by this, as we are providing positive role models and are able to work with our trainees in a supportive and caring manner. Having personal experience of the problems facing women when dealing with New Technology is a vital requirement for the job. All the posts are full-time and the child-care co-ordinator job is an integral part of our team.

The Courses

Courses in micro-electronics and computing training for sixty women were originally due to start in October 1982, but the requisite exemption from the Sex Discrimination Act of 1975 to provide this positive discrimination in technology training for women was delayed beyond our expectations. The Department of Employment seemed unwilling to commit itself to giving exemption from the S.D.A. to a Council, as this was not something they had done before. Their concern appeared to be with the possibility that this "power" might be abused and the exemption applied to other courses and jobs! Until we received official notification of designation from the Department, we could neither publicise our courses nor plan a start-date. This made recruitment of trainees rather problematic. However, in the short time we had for this we proved a great need for our courses and were over-subscribed.

The main aims of the courses are:-
— To get women with few or no qualifications into traditionally male occupations.
— To enable women with children to train to become skilled members of the workforce.
— To provide women with positive role models in traditionally male areas of learning.
— To give women a positive and encouraging environment in which to learn.

In the first course, 50% of the young women's intake had no previous employment experience whatsoever and 50% had had some experience of casual work and work experience programmes. Many of the older women had not worked for some years, whilst others had been employed in part-time, low-paid jobs as cleaners etc. At the time of recruitment, women were either unemployed or in jobs where they were threatened with redundancy.

Our Trainees

The centre's catchment area is South Leeds. We aim to recruit most of our 60 trainees, per course, from this section of Leeds. Much of this area is inner city; it was the main industrial area of Leeds and now has a high rate of unemployment. Response for the first two courses has left us severely over-subscribed. Women are given places on the courses according to their need as single parents, disadvantaged groups, etc.

Advertising of the courses is spread throughout the community venues in the area; rent and rate offices, careers and job centres, etc. Many of the women who come on the courses have, however, heard of the Centre through friends. Meeting women who wish to take the courses takes up much of our time in the summer months. Each woman is invited to the Centre so that she can find out what the course entails. At this meeting each woman talks to at least one of the staff to discuss with her any details of the course or the trainee's needs.

We have made a special priority of the recruitment of women from ethnic minorities and disabled women. Having said this, of course, policy statements have to be put into practice: so we work in conjunction with a community centre to encourage the female Asian centre users to consider our courses. Early recruitment of these trainees is organised so that they can be provided with pre-course study help in English, study techniques and so on. This support continues throughout the course, in the form of a weekly session taught by a tutor from the community centre. This has proved to be of great benefit: we seek to further such links wherever possible. Recruitment of disabled women tends to be arranged through contacts with careers advisers, the equal opportunity officer for the disabled, disabled advisers and social workers for the disabled.

Policies are not enough for the encouragement of disabled women either. The recruitment of disabled women is arranged as far in advance as possible too, so that any adaptations of equipment which might be required can be provided. We have found that there is very little equipment readily available to assist the disabled to work in technological areas. What equipment there is appears to be expensive. Investigations are currently being made to further our plans to provide greater facilities for disabled women in our workshops.

Of the 60 women who began the current course in October 1983, 25% were women from ethnic minority groups and 5% were disabled women. These statistics reflect the mix of the racial groups in South Leeds. We seek to ensure that the number of women from disadvantaged groups is maintained at this level, or improved.

The Teaching Approach

In designing the courses, we take into account the particular problems of women facing the challenges of a new career in computing and electronics. We are aware that many girls at school are not given sufficient encouragement to choose scientific or technical subjects and that at worst they may be actively discouraged by pressure from parents, teachers or peers, from specialising in these areas. This results in a lack of confidence and under-achievement, making many women doubt their own abilities. For all our trainees, taking our courses will mean learning or re-learning study skills, while often having to combine these new patterns of study with their domestic responsibilities. It will mean finding the confidence to tackle new technical subjects and not be put off by any difficulties they encounter.

Sweet Street High Technology Training Centre provides courses where a women-only training environment prevails, where women can find the necessary encouragement and practical support to overcome the disadvantages we have recognised. They do not find themselves in a tiny minority, nor do they receive negative criticism from other trainees or staff. The staff act as positive role models to demonstrate that women can and do achieve an expertise in electronics and computing, given the opportunity.

We have approached this teaching challenge in two ways: primarily by as much emphasis as possible being placed on "hands on" practical work so that the trainees are able, from the first day, to see real results for their efforts — a computer program which runs correctly, a functioning electronic device. Secondly, theory is not taught in large chunks — we teach in both an informal "lecture" style and in "discussion group" style, but all theory is clearly presented as a background to the practical work.

The second important factor in teaching is the group size. We keep classes small and encourage the women to work in twos and threes together. This not only gives support but enables the women to progress at *their* pace. Women are encouraged to work at their individual level without pressure: help is always available in small groups or for the individual woman.

In addition, each woman is assigned her own personal tutor. She is responsible, together with the trainee, for her personal support and guidance and together they are concerned with her progress. The personal tutor has a tutorial group which consists of trainees who are not necessarily taught together. The tutor sees her own students individually, on a regular basis and arranges specific help where needed: tutors use some group-work and counselling techniques in these sessions. It is often in these periods that feelings of self-worth and confidence are explored.

The Computing Course

We feel that the provision of equipment which would closely approximate to that used in industry is vital for our courses. The machine we use, in the main, is a mini-computer with 25 terminals attached. This gives users a fast response time when keying in, editing, compiling or running programs. The computer is a type which is widely used in programming environments. This is a great advantage as it provides credibility for our courses with potential employers.

The purchase of the equipment for the women's courses was not without some anxious moments as it was evident that the need for high quality machines on which to teach was not accepted throughout the Council. We have since purchased additional microcomputers and this seemed to take far longer to be agreed by the appropriate agents than other schemes experienced. It is difficult not to be of the opinion that the courses are regarded as 'temporary' and that the women's courses' right to good equipment is not inalienable.

The course starts by familiarising the trainees with the equipment and easing them into feeling comfortable with the environment. Most will have seen computers before but few will have taken an active role and *used* one. Very few women regard computers that they have at home as theirs, rather than their partner's or children's. Few women get the encouragement at school to learn about using technology and computer groups are usually male dominated. Computers become the province of the male and women's fears about breaking the computer are commonplace so our women are gently encouraged to try to write and experiment with simple programs.

The examples used in teaching are always related to women's experiences in life generally. In this way we are able to encourage the development of confidence and skills, working from what the women are able to do and understand already.

All the course material is written by tutors. We have not found any books or manuals which actually begin at a level which is not intimidating: additionally few books manage to include women in a sufficiently high and positive profile for staff to feel that the effects brought about by their use would have other than a negative value. There is a desperate shortage of material which does start at an appropriate level of understanding and includes examples which do relate to people's, but especially women's experiences. It seems that most women's courses do write their own teaching material: our problem is a common one!

As the trainees gain in confidence and develop their skills, they are introduced to the language of BASIC. This language is taught as it is very commonly used on mini and micro-computers. It is a language which is frequently taught as an introduction to computing for the language's commands and structures, which limit the way that the programmer can arrange the instructions to the computer, are relatively simple. It is introduced through a description of the language's commands and systems. Further theory of the structure and architecture of computers and the relations of the "hardware" are combined in sessions as the women develop programming skills.

Work in the computer language COBOL forms the next section of the course. It is a language used in large commercial concerns and as we intend our trainees to finish the course with experience in a commercial environment and to enter employment as traineee programmers learning COBOL is appropriate. Throughout this section of the course and elsewhere the connections with "real-life" programming are used and all the projects simulate programming projects in business.

In addition, any trainees who show exceptional ability in programming are taught "C" and Unix, a 'state of the art' language and an operating system both of which are rapidly gaining popularity. We are confident that this will make a significant increase to the number of jobs our current trainees will gain at the end of their training course.

Basic mathematics is taught and utilized in the course and many women have found that they enjoy trying out problems that they previously felt unable to do; in a different and more relaxed environment many have found success in this area.

The Electronics Course

As with the computing course, staff have found very little suitable material for use on this course. All the explanatory material is written by staff; although formulae and theory are well-tried and tested, presentation in currently available written material is male-biased. In the staff's experience no book on electronics makes use of a pronoun other than the male "he"! Books for simple electronics circuits for children make such comments as "This circuit will let you know when it is raining. Your mother might find it useful when she has some washing hanging out". Comments such as these are rather disparaging to the mothers building the circuits as they suggest that mothers have no positive role in electronics except as consumers.

The examples we use to demonstrate concepts in electronics are devised to relate as far as possible to the women's everyday lives. The course begins with plug wiring and general explanations about electricity and the laws which govern its use and safety. No prior knowledge on the part of the women is assumed.

Through an emphasis on practical work, the women are taught to build circuits; each woman has her own equipment for these practicals and they generally work individually or in small groups of two or threes.

During practical sessions, the women are taught basic constructional skills so that they can build electronic equipment from circuit diagrams.

The women are taught digital electronics as the final section of the course.

Both Courses

During their courses, the women transfer to the other option and either learn how to program or find out the fundamentals of electronics. So the two month transfer period assures each woman of an all-round basic knowledge of micro-electronics; the link between the hardware and the programming or software is made. We feel that this mixing of the subjects is vital. In this way we can teach the technological background to micro-electronics giving our women confidence and understanding of the relationship of the two elements.

The final three months of the year-long course are spent on an industrial placement with a local company. These are carefully selected, assessed and monitored. The placement period allows the women to develop and augment the skills learnt in the Centre and make contacts with local companies. These contacts are maintained by tutors in order that trainees are assisted in their search for work.

Basic Business Skills

This is the section of the course where the trainees are given help with "return to work" skills, such as how to read a job advert, telephone techniques when ringing up about vacancies, how to fill in an application form, how to write a curriculum vitae and interview techniques.

In addition, we also aim to broaden the experience of the trainees by having a range of visiting speakers at the Centre to talk about such topics as setting up a business and arranging the funding for it, what co-ops are and how they work, talks on the economy of the area, welfare rights, insurance and tax, and so on.

There is also a fairly detailed introduction to bookkeeping, covering what credit and debit mean, and other accounting terms, such as "day book", "sales ledger" and so on. This is particularly helpful to the trainees studying computing, as they are usually expected to be familiar with the financial structures of the organisations for which they work. But in the long term it is expected to benefit all the trainees, especially if, in the current climate of unemployment, they decide to set up their own businesses.

The Process Of 'Selection'

All women who apply to us for a place are supplied with information about the Centre and the courses and we ask for their name, number of children and ages, recent employment history, educational qualifications (if any), courses after leaving school (if any), and any contact with computers or electronics. All these questions are phrased so as to not discourage women who do not have formal qualifications, as our aim is to recruit these women; women under 30 with 'A' level qualifications are not generally offered a place. This is because other courses such as full-time higher education, or TOPS courses are open to them: we aim to provide places for women who have no other route to training, whether because they are over the age limit, have childcare needs, or have no qualifications.

Interviews are then arranged, in groups of six women, general information about our work is given together with a look around, then two staff chat to an individual applicant. This talk includes giving them an idea of the course content and trying to ascertain whether they have a preference for computing or electronics. During this time we try to discover the applicants' attitude to arithmetic by asking them some questions on fractions and some on basic mathematics. We try to assess their general suitability to the courses and to ascertain whether any gap in basic maths can be filled by teaching. Interest and very general educability is sufficient for us to consider an applicant for the course. We usually teach the applicants to add fractions as this is an area which we have found promotes a blank response in most women!

Following the interview, the staff give careful consideration to each applicant and we decide whether or not to offer her a place.

During the induction period before the courses start properly, much time is spent with the childcare co-ordinator organizing childminding and other arrangements. It is essential that these are arranged as early as possible so that the women can relax in the knowledge that their children will not be adversely affected by the course. Financial arrangements often have to be made with women also — many have never had a bank account and as their training allowance is paid in the form of a weekly cheque they are required to open an account.

Financial Arrangements

All arrangements for childcare are paid from the courses' childcare budget. This year's funding incorporates a budget for payment of a trainee allowance of £40 a week with an additional £5 for travel. Many women are still able to claim rates and rent aid, Family Income Supplement and other benefits. They are assisted in this by our link with the unemployed centre in Leeds, whose staff come in to advise the trainees on an individual basis.

Childcare

Without childcare, most of our trainees would be unable to attend our courses. It is an integral part of our facilities. It was an early decision not to provide a creche for children on the Centre's site. This decision was reached because we wished as far as possible to assist women to make arrangements which could be continued after completing the course. The childcare co-ordinator maintains a close link with staff running council nurseries in the city and helps place children under school age at these nurseries. Insufficient nursery places exist: many women have to leave their children with minders. Unless members of the direct family, these childminders have to be registered with Social Services for payment to be arranged.

Children of school age are not omitted from the co-ordinator's planning. Arrangements for after school care are made and paid for if necessary - rather than an after-school club because the children are spread out across the city. Playschemes are arranged for children during school holidays or occasions when schools are closed. Sixty women are currently being trained and their need for playschemes is represented by 40 children between the ages of 5 and 14. The number of children placed in nurseries and with childminders is 16.

As so few nurseries are available it is often difficult for women to gain the places they need for their children. Nurseries often differ with regard to the manager's attitude to the courses too. During the period of placement some make delivering the children and picking them up again in the evening, after work, problematic. Some women have difficulty in adjusting to leaving their children in the care of others. This is more often the case when childminders, rather than nurseries are used because the mothers feel the staff in nurseries to be more 'expert' childcarers.

Employment Prospects

We cannot say for certain yet what success our current trainees will have when they finish the course and look for jobs, but we do have hard figures for our last course. Then, because no training allowance was paid, only 42 trainees out of the 60 who started finished the course. Of those 42, 30 are now in full-time employment, while another two have part-time work as computing tutors. An analysis of these figures is given below. It can be said without exaggeration that all these women have got their jobs because of our course — they were all unemployed before they started, and they have few, if any, qualifications.

While 30 women were initially studying Electronics and 30 studying Computer Programming, 24 completed the Computer Programming course with only 18 completing the Electronics course, a measure of the fact that Electronics is a much harder discipline for women to accept that they can achieve success in.

Of the 24 who completed the Computing course, 19 now have full-time jobs, with another 2 working part-time as Computing Tutors. Of the remaining 19, 3 work as freelance programmers, 2 work as computing tutors (one being a senior tutor in an Information Technology Centre or ITEC), 1 works with computer-aided design, 2 work with data bases, 1 is a computer operator and the remainder are junior programmers.

Of the 18 Electronics trainees, 12 now have full-time jobs. Of these, 2 work as laboratory technicians, 2 teach in an ITEC, 1 services and maintains printers, 3 service and maintain computer peripherals, 1 works in assembly, 1 is a medical technician and the remaining 2 work in the field of radio and TV.

In addition, the women who are still unemployed are, with one exception, all studying for further qualifications, either at the Polytechnic, at Kitson College, or at other futher education colleges in the city.

One former trainee is due to start a Postgraduate Course in Computing in October, and her only qualification is a single 'O' level, and, of course, what she learned here.

Other former trainees have found that their expectations have been heightened; no longer are they content to take basic jobs when they know they can do much better. One woman at interview said that she was so frightened of the Polytechnic that she did not dare enter the doors — she now works there as a technician!

Women on the courses have made various comments:

"I've found I can do sums and things."

"This course has brought me alive."

"Before I came here, I got divorced and then just sat at home doing nothing. My lad started school and I had nothing to do all day. I could have got a job but because of childcare I couldn't. This course is one thing I can do. When I saw the ad, I wanted to learn something worthwhile."

Comments like these make the staff feel that the courses and the hard work are definitely worthwhile. We feel that our "success stories" have been many and varied — for example, a small group of women who had always had difficulties with maths asked if we could arrange a class so they could take 'O' level, and this was an enormous step forward, both for them and for us. But the relationships made with the women and the rewards that these bring on a daily basis are the real incentives to work in what will remain a difficult field for women for many years.

References
1. Office of Population Censuses and Surveys, Statistics Economically Active, 1981 Census.
2. Ursula Huws, "Your Job in the 80's".
3. op.cit. reference 1.
4. idem.
5. idem.

Bibliography

1. *'Balancing the Equation* — a study of women and science and technology within further education.' August 1981. Publication of the *Further Education Curriculum Review and Development Unit.*
2. Women on MSC craft courses. An evaluation of three experimental skill centre courses for women. Michael Nicol, September 1982.
3. *'Practical Approaches to Women's Career Development'* Conference, Report 1981. Manpower Services Commission.

4. 'Getting on in Engineering: Becoming a Female Technician' Peggy Newton and Jeanette Brocklesby, September 1982. Report to Equal Opportunities Commission, from Social Science Research Council Panel on Women and Underachievement.
5. Ursula Huws, 'Your Job in the 80's'.

CHAPTER NINE

Making the Rungs on the Ladder: Women and Community Work Training

Hilary Armstrong.

Not all women community workers feel that community work qualifications are important: not all women community workers appreciate the different class experience contained within women's education. This chapter will argue that one of the most significant issues for working class women community workers in their experience of education is contained within the fears and successes of 'passing' and 'achieving' a qualification. It will try and demonstrate how this experience is vital for those women who have a background of 'failure' in education institutions and can lead to a transformation in the way in which powerful institutions are worked with.

The bulk of the chapter will be detailing the specific nature of one community work course and its attempts to come to terms with working class women's education. However, both in this introduction and in the concluding section I will extrapolate from this specific story to look more generally at the issues involved.

Some of these issues may be surprising to some readers. This surprise should be tempered by remembering both the origins of the writer and the course in question. The North-East of England is very different from either Metropolitan London or other heartlands of the women's movement. It represents a culture and a history where the experience of class runs inevitably through every single aspect of experience.

When, therefore, any aspect of this cultural experience is translated out of this region it is necessary to use the phrase 'working class' as an adjective in most sentences. This is much more than semantics; it is essential to this chapter. For I am discussing the way in which women community activists from communities that can only understand the world in working class ways, come to terms with the state educational institution of a Polytechnic. They do not do so simply for a 'qualification' in some crude materialist fashion; instead the experience of struggling and gaining that qualification plays an important role in changing the women concerned. I will suggest that this experience is significantly different from that of a community worker who attained 4 'A' levels at 18, a degree at 21, and now derides the importance of qualifications as an irrelevance to 'real education' and 'being a community worker'.

The chapter, then, celebrates the importance of a return to a state education institution; the struggle for a 'real' qualification, and the difficulties of that experience for working class women. As such it argues for a structure both in approach to the education of working class community activists, and in the struggle for women's confidence and political growth.

The Struggle for Certification

The course at Sunderland Polytechnic began in 1975. A decade ago, attacking state institutions was a normal feature of all discussions of community work. The early CDP reports; the successful inner city struggles; the miners (twice) were all underlining a progress in the practice of struggle against the state. Against this background, certification seemed a reactionary thing; inessential to the real way forward; a 1950s sort of thing which was not 'really' necessary in engaging with the 'real' struggles of working class experience. Consequently one of the main discussions within the group setting up such a course is to be found in the very nature and existence of the course itself. OK then, if at the very end we *have* to start a course; and if we *have* to have it certified, then we will minimise precisely those elements of it which stress the institution and the certification. It will be loose; it will be unstructured; it will *have* to have *some* assessment but really, if we all had our way (or at least what passed for our way in the middle 1970's) we would have minimised both the structures and the assessment out of existence.

Any course setting up in Sunderland had to take account of the reality of poor school achievement, alongside a decline in traditional industries which was yet another contribution to the devastation of local inner city areas. We also could not ignore the fact that many community activists were women. The course, therefore, consciously set out to tackle these bits of reality in the admissions policy, in the structure and process of the course, and in the assessment system. It has meant that in almost every year group there has been a majority of women, with formal recognisable academic qualification not being the main criteria for acceptance. We have always tried to value what people have done in their lives, rather than what certificates they can produce. However, this has often meant an enormous struggle for the students, who feel they have nothing against which to value their experience; they were only getting on with life. They had got involved with playschemes because that was the only way to keep the bairns occupied in the holidays, and as for the tenants association, well, when the repairs weren't done, and you couldn't get anybody at the council to listen, what would you have done?

The course is a two year full-time one leading to a professional qualification in Youth and Community Work: it is a recognisable entry into paid work with people, traditionally in youth centres and community centres, but latterly accepted by a much broader group of employers in the community and youth work arena. The Sunderland Course has become acknowledged as one way in which local activists, volunteers, and part-time workers can have useful, relevant training, leading to a recognisable qualification, even if they have not passed exams at school, or had any experience of Further Education. The intake has varied over the years from eighteen to twenty four students, but we have always had a number who have come without any acknowledged academic background.

From the beginning then, there have been two particular influences which have continued to be reflected in the aims, structure and content of the course: regional developments and specific educational considerations. Regional developments have always been a consideration; the processes of change associated with de-industrialisation have created severe problems around unemployment, urban decay, and poverty. This has led to significant change in the social and cultural relationships of the area.

Educational disadvantage in the North-East is well documented. Government statistics record a poor rate of secondary continuance after 16, comparatively low rates of academic attainment, and poor entry and progression into further and higher education. They also record that educational disadvantage is felt particularly by the female population, who are also of course, likely to be the largest group of people actually involved in community groups.

A conscious attempt has been made to take these factors into account through trying to use particular teaching methods appropriate to meeting the problems of adult educational disadvantage, through consideration of theory and practice relevant to the sociology of the area, and through a course structure which permits a high degree of student participation.

I moved to teach on the course in 1975 from a neighbourhood community work post in the town, where I had worked with the usual range of groups on the usual range of issues. This was different. Much of the 'success' and 'failure' in the neighbourhood job had been around issues that crucially affected the women's daily lives, but where there were clear external factors at play. Also, the struggles around these issues were very much collective experiences. Higher education brought different experiences; success and failure was inevitably much more individualised, and however much the group experience of the course, or of parts of the course was enjoyable and offered opportunities for collective working, at the end of the day students were on their own at assessment.

In the early days, I did not fully appreciate these differences, and underestimated the importance of working class women struggling, through higher education, with the largely negative experience of their early education, and the different, contrasting experience of community activity which had brought them to college. By trying to run the course in the loosely structured, collective way that community workers who worked with groups in the community employ we did not take seriously enough the legacy of those early educational experiences, and the effect of that on an individual's self-image.

The balance of process and end suddenly seemed much more precarious. It was not possible to allow the groups to develop at their own pace — that could take longer than the two years, and the sense of individual failure would then be intensified. However, to concentrate purely on individual advancement without concern for the process, would be to run an academic course with little relevance to the values of youth and community work that we wanted to support. That would also mean that in selecting students we would have to take those applicants who we knew could survive in that sort of race. In reality that was never an option we considered.

Our expectations as staff were constantly challenged by students, and this chapter comes from the learning that I have gone through in facing these issues. Undoubtedly, some of the assumptions that were current in community work that I took to the course have been severely challenged. The movement and change is not over. Hopefully some of our lessons will be at least a contribution to the debate.

One of the first challenges was on 'standards'. We said in the early days that the main criteria for assessment would be a student's *own* development, — not their progress as compared to others on the course. Did this then mean that everyone would pass? It was very painful for the staff to be really clear about this: that there were some people who, no matter what individual progress was made, would not *Pass*. I remember long meetings, with students and with other members of the department, where these issues were thrashed out, with a massive fear lurking under the surface: is it possible for *anyone* to get this qualification? We moved as if over egg shells towards talking about standards, towards establishing criteria for measurement. But we did that in a way that involved students in a real sense in the discussion, and in sharing accountability for the way that standards were set, and assessed. The experience of the assessment system involves students in clarifying *what* is being assessed, as well as in *how* it is assessed. They work with staff on assessment panels, and far from this being an easy cop-out, it is a challenging, nerve-wracking experience. But it also provides a structure for discussing work openly with colleagues, and for support for colleagues to be demonstrated in a very real way.

The open debate about this, the continuing (although often contradictory) pressure from fieldworkers, meant that we developed much greater clarity about what we meant by standards, and about just what it is that a community and youth worker needs to know, and needs to be able to do, and how far 'personal' qualities are involved. The fact that these issues were the subject of discussion among students did two things. Firstly it demystified the whole area: such things weren't the sole property of staff. Secondly it highlighted the fact that the area of 'standards' was as much part of process as anything else. In other words the definition of 'good' youth and community practice in 1974 had moved and changed by 1984. For example sexism and racism were issues largely regarded as marginal in 1974, whereas in 1984 even in the Andy Capp, white North East, those issues and how workers tackle them both as workers and as individuals, are central. A student who dismisses consideration of race or of gender in their work will invite criticism from peers as well as from staff and field workers.

To work within a world that is quite obviously *not* static, and to therefore deal with the realisation that intervention in that world has to also move and change can be quite threatening: as more than one student has said, the problem with the course is that it makes it very clear that you are never 'there'; that you have always in our field to open yourself up to the new challenges, to conflicting views, and to personal change. However, in order to deal with this constant change, there had to be a framework of stability. In the real world outside of college, everything is not constantly on offer: why would it be on a course? Suspicion was there when we tried to say students could decide, and of course, once again, the students were right.

An important development in the course has been the recognition of the different position of staff and students, of men and women and of black and white on the course. In trying to develop open and democratic ways of working, we had to recognise that particular groups and individuals on the course had different amounts of power and influence, and that to pretend that everyone was equal was to perpetuate the differences as inequalities. The specific attention to gender arose out of this lesson. We certainly did not start with a conscious feminist objective; we did start with a determination to offer appropriate training for working class people in the North East, and with a determination that we would open up those opportunities for women. But that determination had to be translated into the curriculum, and more importantly the structure of the course. In the first year we had eight women out of 24 students in all.

Men's Experience

I had been used to working with men as colleagues and managers, but had enjoyed working with groups of women in the community in ways that I only began to fully recognise when I was suddenly confronted with a largely male-dominated group. I missed the openness, the commitment to just getting on with things; I was bewildered by the formality that some of the male working-class students expected in procedures, and by the way that some of the women reverted to subordinate roles in the large group. Many of the men coming on to the Sunderland Course are coming to terms with redundancy, but will have had experience of some position of status in their lives as chair of the Tenant's Association, shop steward, councillor, magistrate. This often means that they have a carefully constructed self-image which leads to a resistance to challenge. They come wanting a qualification for a job (which has frequently anyway been seen as a soft touch to the real job they were doing in the shipyards, or the steel works), and are not prepared for the personal challenge that a professional course inevitably involves.

The support and confidence building that I was used to developing with women was sometimes counter-productive with the men, and very difficult with the women students when they were outnumbered by men who, for all sorts of understandable reasons, could not allow the women to move and grow, without themselves feeling under threat. It all sounds so obvious now, but the important inequalities in gender relationships in working class communities do not suddenly disappear on a course in higher education. The anxiety around returning to education was an additional pressure on this. For most of the men, they had never had to think about the way they related to women as being oppressive, and certainly did not expect that sort of thing to be an issue on a course. While some working class men do get more involved in child care and family responsibilities as a response to unemployment, frequently the reaction is to hold on to 'maleness' as the only area of themselves that they can retain control of. So some men on the course were angry about any challenge to the personal areas of their life. Others of course were already struggling with such challenges, and continued to do so on the course.

Women's Experience

However, it was much more difficult for women to separate out what was happening to them on the course and what was happening in their lives. Feminism has enabled us to link those things that have always been regarded as private — 'the personal' — to what is going on in state institutions, to political and economic life. The saying attributed to Lenin: 'everything is related to everything else' suddenly takes on a new, and overpowering meaning. Women coming on the course were faced with the knowledge that they were stepping outside of the normal activity of women in their neighbourhood, and of their class, that they were challenging the accepted roles of wives and mothers, and they were doing it by the simple but mammoth step of going into a course in an institution of higher education. In that act alone they were making a statement to their husbands, their children and their neighbours, but most of them depended on these very people for support while on the course. That meant that they could not separate how they saw themselves as women from how they saw themselves as wives and mothers, how they saw themselves as community activists, and as students. When I've talked to past women students, particularly in connection with this chapter, their over-riding impression is of going through enormous personal change, while other people in the family watched with bewilderment. The change was exciting, interesting, often painful. But it had to be tempered with the material reality that surrounded them. For some women, the course provided the springboard for dramatic changes in their personal life. Most women have continued to live with their families in their working-class neighbourhoods, but with an understanding of what is going on in that neighbourhood, and in the lives of their friends, that is clearly reflected in the sort of work they are now able to do.

The strength of women on the course has grown. It has grown with the course being able to tackle more effectively through the structure of the course, through the assessment system, the inequalities that women have experienced. They are strengthened because they remain in day-to-day contact with their community, with the people who make up their background, and the reality of that is brought into college.

But women's strength is also, and essentially, developed through a closer attention to the detail of learning, to structure, to writing, to assessment, to validation, than we acknowledged in the early days.

The struggle around writing is a good example of this. It is so easy when trying to encourage the educationally disadvantaged, to undervalue the importance of practitioners being able to deal effectively with the written word, and the importance in training of being able to explore a variety of ideas and concepts. Students need to understand and develop their own conceptual framework in order to make intervention meaningful. This cannot be done without being able to have confidence in reading and criticising what others have written, or without working out your own ideas in written work, and therefore allowing others to read and criticise your work. This has meant a variety of approaches on the course, and we are still trying out new ideas. All students do study skills in the first year. Some individual students with particular difficulties will be given additional personal tuition, whereas others are encouraged to join writing groups or other further education classes. Some applicants are accepted on condition that they agree to do some tutored preparatory work in this area before coming on the course, whereas others we advise to apply the following year after doing some work to develop their literacy skills.

This is obviously very haphazard, and also time-consuming for the staff, and therefore not always as thorough, or as effective as it ought to be. This means that we are currently looking at the possibility of developing access courses with local colleges of further education. The argument has been put that we would simply be putting another hurdle in the way of working class people gaining entry into higher education. However, evidence from elsewhere in the country suggests that probably the opposite is true. Certainly 'writing' is the area of the course that raises the most anxiety, and around which a lot of confidence, or lack of it, revolves. When a student who has been outside formal education for fifteen to twenty years experiences success in the academic area, that is cause for real celebration.

In an area like the North East, where work opportunities have considerably diminished, the pressure on those leaving the course to get a job so as to prove to their families and friends that the pain and sacrifice have been worthwhile is very strong. Amazingly, the employment record for students leaving the course is very high. For the women in particular, it is often not possible for them to leave the area and so they have to look for jobs locally. This means that not only do they have to do the course under the gaze of family and friends, but do their job under those same critical eyes. The expectations in this situation are very conflicting: that the new worker will not have changed, will not have moved from the working class, but at the same time will have moved, and will be bringing new expertise and understanding to the job. This area in itself is a very painful struggle for students; frequently their main motivation is to work within their own communities, but training seems to set them apart. It would be silly of me to pretend that every student has worked this out in a way that is satisfactory to them; for the occasional student it has led to disenchantment. For other students, that very process has been a significant area of movement. One worker who left the course two years ago to return to the work she had left, came to see me recently to discuss a new area of work she is going to move into. She is now happy that she has met her obligations, but that also, another member of the group she is working with is now confident enough to take over her role and responsibilities. She rightly experiences this as a great success; she has been able to move, but not to be seen as rejecting the position she came from.

Why is it that in 1975 we wanted to throw structure, assessment, standards out of the window?

Well, firstly, we believed that working class community activists, particularly women, were very frightened of education. We saw that they had been very badly treated in the previous experience of education and that therefore they rejected and feared that structure of education. We therefore, wrongly, felt that an unstructured approach to the educational process was correct.

Secondly, we saw that their educational experience had been dominated by assessment and examinations, that this experience had, for them, led to the inevitable linking between education, assessment and failure, and that therefore they were afraid of all such links. We therefore again came to the wrong conclusion that they were against certification, hurdles and examination.

What then is the relationship between these rights and wrongs? The answer lies in a misreading of the social relationships of working class material experience of education. Education is, for the working class, not simply an *experience* which is rejected as nasty and then forgotten. Education is a set of institutions which distribute resources in society. It is impossible to 'reject' education; as impossible as it is to 'reject' money. It exists and continues to exist in working class life long after the kids have slunk out of the school gates for that last exulting time. That is not the 'end of education' for the rest of their lives, the paper is opened up at the 'jobs' page and qualifications are viewed; the job shop has qualifications on all its adverts — the friend from school who went off comes back richer. Their own children start school, and they are faced with helping them to read, with going to parents evenings. Education is part of the normal experience of everyday life. Working class women cannot forget it. They can stifle the experience, the sense of failure in themselves; but they are reminded materially of it everyday in a million ways.

What goes on in such experience then? There is an awful contradiction, a contradiction mirrored in many other areas of working class life. This or that bit of the world is *both* very painful *and* very important. For those with money, power and confidence it is possible to extricate themselves from this contradiction by rejecting such areas of experience. For working class women education remains something with a tremendous social and material power, something to be derided, something to be feared, something to be achieved. When the chance comes to re-enter, of course it will be rejected initially as not for me. Indeed who willingly will enter such an experience, such a painful memory. On the other hand who can simply reject it or dismiss it as it exists so powerfully within working class material experience.

Education is opportunity; it is also a painful memory. To fail to underline the way in which it is opportunity is to fail to mesh in with the reality of working class life. To fail to understand the pain of that past failure is *also* to fail to understand working class life. It is essential then to combine both in your curriculum structure and pedagogy. For this certification, assessment achievement, success and failure are essential; *not* because the validating bodies say so, but because the social relations of working class life demand it.

Afterword

"Education is, for the working class, not simply an experience which is rejected as nasty then forgotten. Education is a set of institutions which distribute resources in society." This quote from Chapter 9 sums up why community workers must be concerned with education. Education as a set of institutions governing the distribution of resources is an area that has not so far had the attention it deserves, although the methods and philosophy of non formal education have greatly influenced community work practice.

Common underlying themes emerge clearly from many of the chapters; the need for women to be together apart from men, the crucial need for childcare. Other themes are either implicit or are raised but not necessarily answered within the book. What do we mean by education? It is used both to signify non formal learning experience in all its many forms and formally recognised learning which is often needed as a means to securing employment, status and economic independence. Yet it would be invidious to divorce these two entirely from each other; indeed Hilary Armstrong's chapter describes a continued effort to translate women's (and men's) learning experiences into a formal qualification. The chapters encompass many types of learning such as theatre, role play and community action and raise questions as to how we can get these experiences credited as "real" learning within the system and whether such accreditation is necessary.

The book falls into two distinct sections: what we call "mainstream" provision and "compensatory" education. Mainstream covers school, careers and further education; compensatory deals with youth work, adult education and alternative training.

This raises the whole issue of how much we should be trying to provide alternatives and how much we are about providing access to mainstream education. For, whilst we would wish to assert the fundamental importance of individual and collective learning in their own right, we have to recognise that success at mainstream education is a gateway to jobs that few of those we work with can afford to reject. And, in recognising the role mainstream education plays in society, we would wish to challenge and change its values, content and methods; an increasingly hard task in the current political climate. Yet the very difficulty of present times makes it a more necessary task. At a conference held in Durham in 1984, one of the speakers said how the last ten years had seen womens education "move from a position of precarious marginality to one of permanent marginality." The last year on Tyneside has seen that position shifted back to one of precariousness as full time permanent posts in women's education are not filled when vacancies arise and more and more of the work is done by people on short term contracts. As the room to move on the margins gets increasingly less, so there is a greater need to tackle the centre and challenge the way the provision and development of mainstream services often benefits neither women nor the working class. And for those of us who have worked on the "margins" there is also a need to find ways of using the skills and confidence we have gained to make an assault on the establishment.

Clearly the extensive gender socialisation, described so graphically by Val Millman, is so deeply rooted in family, school and public life that it will take a very sustained and massive shift to change things for the bulk of girls and women. Because many women go through school and initial careers advice with very traditional ideas about their role in life, there is an ever present need for wider educational opportunities later on in life. Hence the importance of the involvement of many women with schemes such as the EEC's non traditional skills courses, particularly now that apprenticeships, never of easy access for women, have virtually dried up. "Compensatory" initiatives will continue to be needed as a vital part of providing opportunities for at least some girls and women. Identifying scope for such initiatives, in alliance where possible with school staff, must be a concern for every community worker, whether at neighbourhood or district level. But these initiatives must always be seen also as a base from which we can attack the core.

Tackling mainstream education is a more difficult issue but not one we would wish to see community workers duck. Val Millman has identified numerous ways in which, from her standpoint as a teacher, she can see opportunities to form alliances with resource people from outside; community workers are potentially a major resource here. Through contact with parents and other professionals with whom the school may, or could, work community workers are in a good position to identify where opportunities exist within the school to change its practice or develop new approaches. Linking in with moves to promote anti-racism within the curriculum could prove of great benefit as norms of school and society are questioned. One specific possibility is intervention in governing bodies. Community workers could both seek to involve themselves directly, either through their local activities or trade unions, and could encourage local people to become involved. An important part of the strategy would be the provision of training and organisation of pre-meetings in order to strengthen our effectiveness. There are examples of institutions changing to meet needs more effectively, for example the provision of access courses at some polytechnics, the move to reschedule courses at Lancashire Polytechnic so that they can all be done on a part time basis thus making them accessible to the unemployed, and the move by trade union members of Newcastle Polytechnic Council to get an effective equal opportunities policy. Pressure could be brought to bear to get other institutions to change in such ways.

Judy Seymour's chapter shows the need for community workers to consider seriously what work with men should be about. Many men would claim to be supportive to women's rights but few spend time re-defining their own work with men: what kinds of values should that be supporting? What questions should it ask? Again it highlights the need for a broad attack on all fronts, for without this the small gains we make in one sector cannot make headway against the tide of opposition.

Mary is very clear about the need for good child care if women are to take advantage of education — something we'd all agree with. Yet, whilst no self respecting "alternative" education would fail to consider the provision of child care arrangements, we have failed to make much impact on mainline establishments — in some cases cuts are actually eroding gains previously made. Again, Mary's and Connie's experience of the value of theatre groups in education brings us sharp up against recent cuts in community arts funding, which has been made worse by the abolition of the Metropolitan County Councils and the Greater London Council.

It is important to look not only at the dimension of sex but also of class, another issue raised overtly in the interview with Mary. For middle class women the experience of working with men can be personally difficult and bewildering but it is not often the same kind of paralysing experience that Mary talks of. We need to think very clearly about the kind of support we give women in these situations — for many women the option of staying in exclusively female groups is not there, yet the experience of being in a group with men can undo all the confidence learnt in women's groups unless there is support to work through this.

"Community Education" is another way to go for community workers at a local level; for whilst it is extremely hard to change schools from the outside, supporting alliances with parents and concerned teachers will provide a starting point from which change can develop. And, at a policy level, community workers can campaign for a recognition that sex and race inequality are major issues in education.

What, therefore, are the messages we see emerging from the book. Education is a huge field — after health and social security probably the biggest in the country, and certainly the dominant responsibility amongst all local authority services (unless the Government's present trend of gradually removing bits from local authority control becomes a wholesale takeover.)

Several chapters within the book (Barbara Hancock, Judy Seymour, Hilary Armstrong) indicate how community work theory and practice has grown and enriched itself in the last decade by taking on issues related to women, and in particular, women's education at a variety of practical levels.

Yet there has been a major change in British society which makes this expansion and enrichment all the more important, even though at the same time it means that it hasn't resulted in the gains for women that it otherwise might have. For the progress of women's issues has to be seen in the context of the present political situation, the overriding practical and cultural reductionism of the first and now present Thatcher government. The whole superstructure of British society — systems of health, education, culture and welfare fought for over generations by women and men — is under direct attack. Cash limits, denationalisation, rate-capping: within three broad heads we witness the destruction of the National Health Service, further and higher education, public services in general, telecommunications and even the basis of an industrial society, coal, steel and rail. Whilst women are making some gains it is within a situation where there are increasing attacks on the quality of life of ordinary people and increasingly fewer jobs.

We see government removing the right of opposition, a far cry from the almost halcyon days of the late 1970's when radicals in community work and elsewhere were able to indulge in a critique of the failings of social democracy; to show how successive Labour Governments had betrayed their political base and failed to achieve meaningful change.

"Our intention was to use the enquiry to add to the pressure on the government to change its disastrous policies.... Many of our weaknesses come from a failure to look thoroughly into why Labour Governments have not lived up to the expectations working people have of them. *For this has happened not just once but again and again:* every time in fact. The result has been accumulated cynicism not just about Labour politicians —

as about all politicians — but any form of political action, any collective effort to change things."[1]

"The recent cuts in public expenditure which have affected services, often drastically, have not meant that workers get a refund (from the social wage) in their pay packets; on the contrary their money has been redirected away from services for the working class into bolstering up the production side of the capitalist economy through subsidies of one sort or another to private industry."[2]

But that criticism was apt and important. One of the reasons people have not defended services more strongly is that they never felt they were their services in the first place. Standing our ground, defending the little we have, claiming and fighting for additional resources are important because they are part of the opposition to destruction. But it is important not just to try and return to the old days but rather to lay claim to a new and better future where our needs and those of the people we work with will be met.

In demanding child care as an integral part of continuing education provision; in demanding continuing education itself; in drawing attention to the need for specific resources for work with young women within youth work and careers; in setting up schemes like the Sweet Street Centre, or women's education projects, community workers and others, not least the students and participants, are laying claim to public sector resources which are rightfully ours and, further, are saying to government: "we will have these things despite you".

Thus we acknowledge the opportunities and contradictions afforded by the EEC's Social Fund in funding a high technology training centre for women whilst at the same time imposing quotas on steel, coal and food; quotas geared to the needs of capital rather than people. We also note Minister's comments referred to by Val Millman. While welcoming these at their face value, we contrast the Government's abolition of the Schools' Council and encouragement of the Higher Education Advisory Board, which is set fair to sound the death knell of many courses. Even as the Engineering Industry Training Board is saying it wants to attract women into engineering, that industry is contracting alarmingly.

Rate capping diminishes further the education and schooling systems with which we currently make do. The Manpower Services Commission introduces "Training for Jobs" to replace further education. Objective reality insists that we try to retain and expand the gains — and wonderfully rich and effective work — outlined. And we do this with optimism as well as determination. Our practice is powerful: we stand together for growth, development and change.

References:
1. Coventry, Liverpool, Newcastle and North Tyneside Trades Councils 1980 *State Intervention in Industry: a Workers Inquiry*, p.5 (Revised edition, Spokesman 1982).
2. North Tyneside CDP Final Report Volume 1 1978 *North Shields: Working Class Politics and Housing 1900 — 1977*, p4.

Bibliography

1. WOMEN START HERE PART ONE: HANDBOOK, PART TWO: CASE STUDIES — eds Chris Cherry, Moira Turnbull, Scottish Adult Basic Education Unit. A basic education pack for tutors/ organisers working with women in informal learning groups.
2. GETTING STARTED — A basic education pack for tutors/ organisers working with women in informal learning groups. Workers Education Association
3. WOMEN, CLASS AND ADULT EDUCATION — Jane Thompson, University of Southampton
4. NEW OPPORTUNITIES FOR WOMEN — Ed. Valerie Wilson, Scottish Institute of Adult Education
5. LEADING A GROUP — A WORKSHOP FOR GROUP LEADERS USING COMMUNITY EDUCATION PACKS — Open University 1984 ISBN 0335 15100 0
6. BREAKING OUR SILENCE: AN INTRODUCTION. — Margaret Marshall.FROM A DIFFERENT PERSPECTIVE: CHANGE IN WOMENS EDUCATION. Eileen Aird. WOMEN AT THE CROSSROADS: TEN YEARS OF NEW OPPORTUNITIES FOR WOMENS COURSES IN THE NORTHERN DISTRICT. Freda Tallantyre. All three from Workers Educational Association 1985.
7. I'M A NEW WOMAN NOW: EDUCATION FOR WOMEN IN LIVERPOOL — Liz Cousins, Priority, Liverpool. ISBN 0-9502785-1-3
8. ADULT EDUCATION FOR A CHANGE — Ed. Jane L. Thompson Hutchinson 1980.
9. LEARNING LIBERATION: WOMENS RESPONSE TO MEN'S EDUCATION — Jane Thompson Croom Helm 1983
10. MAKING HISTORY 2: WOMEN — Television History Centre in Association with Channel 4 from THC, 42 Queen Square, London WC1N 3AJ.

11. HERSTUDIES: A SELECTIVE LIST OF RESOURCES ON WOMENS HISTORY AND GENDER — from History and Social Services Teachers Centre, 377 Clapham Road, London. SW9 9BT.
12. WOMEN AND EDUCATION — Eileen Byrne Tavistock Publications 1978.
13. ADULT EDUCATION AND COMMUNITY ACTION Tom Lovett, T. Clarke and Avila Kilmurray Croom Helm 1983.
14. ISSUES IN COMMUNITY EDUCATION C. Fletcher and N. Thompson Falmer Press 1980.
15. CHANGING THE FOCUS: WOMEN AND FURTHER EDUCATION Further Education Unit 1985
16. "BALANCING THE EQUATION" A study of Women and Science and Technology within Further Education. August 1981. Publication of the Further Education Curriculum Review and Development Unit.
17. IT'S NEVER TOO LATE: A PRACTICAL GUIDE TO CONTINUING EDUCTION FOR WOMEN OF ALL AGES. Joan Perkin Impact Books 1984
18. WOMEN ON MSC CRAFT COURSES An evaluation of three experimental skill craft courses for women.
19. PRACTICAL APPROACHES TO WOMEN'S CAREER DEVELOPMENT Conference Report 1981. Manpower Services Commission
20. GETTING ON IN ENGINEERING: BECOMING A FEMALE TECHNICIAN Peggy Newton, Jeanette Brocklesby, September 1982 report to Equal Opportunities Commission. From Social Science Research Council panel on Women and Under-achievement.
21. YOUR JOB IN THE 80'S Ursula Huws
22. WOMEN IN COLLECTIVE ACTION ACW 1982
23. WOMEN IN THE COMMUNITY Mayo RKP
24. THOMPSON REPORT ON THE YOUTH SERVICE IN ENGLAND HMSO 1982
25. DIXON ET AL "FEMINIST PERSPECTIVES AND PRACTICE"? ET AL, COMMUNITY WORK AND THE STATE
26. DEVELOPING ANTI SEXIST INNOVATIONS ILEA 1982
27. JUST LIKE A GIRL Sue Sharpe, Penguin 1976
28. CONTINUING EDUCATION: FROM POLICIES TO PRACTICE Advisory Council for Adult Continuing Education, 1982.
29. ETHNOCENTRISM AND SOCIALIST FEMINIST THEORY by Michele Barrett and Mary McIntosh in *Feminist Review* no.20 (1985).

Contributors

Hilary Armstrong has taught on the Sunderland Polytechnic Youth and Community Work course since 1975. Previously she was a neighbourhood community worker in Sunderland. She is Labour's Prospective Parliamentary Candidate for Durham North-west.

Alicia Bruce is employed as a regional development officer with Community Business Central, working to support women in cooperatives and community enterprise. She previously worked with S.A.B.E.U. (the Scottish Adult Basic Education Unit). She has been active in the women's movement in Scotland since the early 70's and is convenor of the S.I.A.E. National Women and Education Group. She is at present researching into the education of females in 19th century Scotland for a doctoral thesis at the University of Stirling.

Pam Flynn worked for 8 years in theatre marketing and public relations before doing a TOPS - funded Diploma in Adult Education at Liverpool University. She has worked since 1979 for the City of Newcastle's Adult Education Outreach Project, an action-research project into non formal adult education in the inner city.

Olivia Grant began her career in the Careers Service in 1968 and worked in a variety of offices in the north-west of England, including Ashton-under-Lyne, Kirkby and Skelmersdale. In 1974 she became Principal Careers Officer for the newly-formed Borough of Trafford, and in November 1979 she moved to Newcastle-upon-Tyne to take up the post of Principal Careers Officer. She has three children.

Barbara Hancock worked for several years as a neighbourhood community worker before changing to work in women's Second Chance education. Now, with two small children, she has a part-time job back in community work, so is faced with having to test out some of the theories in her chapter!

Chris Johnson has worked as a community worker in both Salford and Newcastle-upon-Tyne. She is now Education Worker for the North East Trade Union Studies Information Unit.

Sue Lieberman (previously Leigh) was Inner City Officer at Newcastle-upon-Tyne Council for Voluntary Service from 1979-85. She has worked both as a neighbourhood community worker and in welfare rights, and lived in the north-east of England for ten years before taking up a post as Development Officer for policy and services with Edinburgh District Council's Women's Committee.

Val Millman has taught in primary and secondary schools, and was Coordinator of the Schools Council Sex-Differentiation Project (1981-83). She has lived and worked in the centre of Coventry since 1974 and is currently leading a three-year curriculum development project on equal opportunities (gender) across Coventry LEA.

Linda Moore began her career in the Careers Service in the London Borough of Croydon in 1974. She continued to work in the south-east until moving to Newcastle at the beginning of 1983, where she took up post as Deputy Principal Careers Officer for the City.

Judy Seymour is 36 years old and has an 11-year old daughter. She was founder member of an all-women community arts group working in the inner city of Newcastle and Gateshead. She coordinates the Tyneside Working with Girls Development Group.

Deborah Trayhurn lives and works in Leeds. Having worked with the GLC, she became interested in computing, retrained and was one of the original members of the Sweet Street staff. She left the Centre in 1984. She still works encouraging women into New Technology areas of work as Admissions Tutor for the computing department at Leeds Polytechnic, and remains closely involved with the work of the women's courses. Other interests include sport: having trained in the first instance as a PE teacher!

Very Nice Work If You Can Get It
The Socially Useful Production Debate
Edited by Collective Design/Projects

Socially Useful Production seeks to join needs with resources. It spans services, products, labour processes, political demands, political theories and social ideas. No single object, movement or project completely contains and delimits the term. Overall, it relates to the specific needs of particular people: young and old; black and white; men and women; fit and unfit; skilled and unskilled; oppressed and liberated.

Many of the contributors to *Very Nice Work* are centrally involved in recent developments that consciously invoke the aims of Socially Useful Production. They report and celebrate a number of important projects, including initiatives by the Greater London Council, Sheffield City Council and the West Midlands County Council. The editors hope it may provide the basis for a strong, exuberant politics and practice which can both challenge the logics that capital deploys and sustain the growth of oppositional visions and forms.

"This book is stimulating and informative. Its ideas may help us towards a socially useful Government".

Audrey Wise

Contributors:

Cliff Allum	Paul Field	Vin McCabe
Erica Carter	Ursula Huws	Seymour Melman
Cynthia Cockburn	Chris Lee	David Noble
Philip Cooke	Sonia Liff	David Pelly
Mike Cooley	John Lovering	Hilary Wainwright

Illustrated 220pp
Paper £4.95
Cloth £17.20

ISBN 0 85124 431 9
ISBN 0 85124 430 0

SPOKESMAN
Bertrand Russell House, Gamble Street, Nottingham, UK
Tel. 0602 708318

Joint Action for Jobs
A New Internationalism
Edited by Ken Coates, with a foreword by Stuart Weir

Unemployment is laying Europe waste. With twenty million people out of work, the number of direct victims has become intolerable: a common scandal. But there is every reason to believe that this number is growing steadily, whilst the direct sufferers already include whole populations. Yet there is no reason to believe that unemployment is unavoidable or foreordained. A mere fraction of the ingenuity which has transformed our technical capacities could re-arrange our social rules in a way which would guarantee a useful role for all our people.

Of course, action by Governments can improve or worsen this condition. If all or even some of the European Governments were willing to act together in order to reject mass unemployment, there is no doubt that conditions could be radically improved. But this is not a problem which can be left to governments. Because it concerns everybody, it needs action by all of us. The work which is necessary requires us to find ways of joining needs to resources, of restructuring institutions to regain the democratic initiative in the global economy. We must find ways to replace the policies of 'beggar my neighbour' by those which seek instead to 'better my neighbour'.

"These excellent essays show how vital it is for socialists who wish to have an impact on unemployment to broaden their horizons, and think internationally".

Ben Pimlott

"Reflecting the thought and experience of those who have already been involved in local enterprise, and building networks to transcend national boundaries, it is an important contribution not only to the debate but to the practical answer to the tens of millions of people without jobs and without the prospect of work in the industrialised world".

David Blunkett

". . . a serious attempt to seek an international solution to some of the major economic problems facing the next Labour Government. It is vital for the Labour Party that it be widely discussed.

Lewis Minkin

Paper £4.95
Cloth £17.50
232pp

ISBN 0 85124 428 9
ISBN 0 85124 427 0

SPOKESMAN
Bertrand Russell House, Gamble Street, Nottingham, UK
Tel. 0602 708318